# NASCAR® RACING

*from*

Papyrus Design Group, Inc.

Copyright ©1994 Papyrus Design Group, Inc., All Rights Reserved. NASCAR Racing is officially licensed by NASCAR.

# Table Of Contents

**Quick Start Guide And In-Car Controls**.................................. 4
   On The Track: A Quick Glance................................ 5
   On The Track: In The Cockpit................................. 7
   The Pit Board............................................................ 12
   Pausing The Action................................................. 13
   Using Your Radio.................................................... 14

**Game Menus And Functions**............................................. 23
   The Main Menu..................................................... 23
   The Single Race Menu........................................... 26
   Championship Season............................................ 29
   Preseason Testing................................................... 32
   Multiplayer Racing................................................. 33
   Driver Info............................................................... 39
   The Options Menu................................................. 40
         Realism.................................................... 42
         Opponents.............................................. 44
         Driving Aids........................................... 46
         Graphics Detail..................................... 47
         Sound..................................................... 50
   Arcade Driving....................................................... 51
   The Instant Replay................................................. 52

**The NASCAR Circuit**........................................................ 58
   Atlanta Motor Speedway........................................ 58
   Bristol International Raceway................................. 61
   Darlington Raceway............................................... 65
   Martinsville Speedway............................................ 68
   Michigan International Speedway.......................... 71
   New Hampshire International Speedway............... 74
   Phoenix International Raceway............................... 77
   Talladega Superspeedway....................................... 80
   Watkins Glen International..................................... 83

# Contents Continued...

**On The Track: Preparing To Win** .......................................... 86

**The Garage Menu** ..................................................................... 96
    NASCAR Tires ............................................................................ 98
    Fuel ............................................................................................ 108
    Spoiler Adjustments ................................................................ 110
    Suspension Science ................................................................ 114
    Gear Ratios .............................................................................. 129
    Options .................................................................................... 131

**American History: Evolution Of NASCAR Racing** ....... 133

**Appendixes** ............................................................................... 166
    Using The Paint Kit ................................................................. 166
    NASCAR Winston Cup Champions ..................................... 176
    Index ......................................................................................... 177

*"Race drivers are schizophrenics...I'm a completely different person outside the car."*

-*NASCAR Great Buddy Baker*

# On The Track: A Quick Glance

If you're like most of us, you don't want to read the instructions, you want to "slide right through the window" and drive the race car. For this reason, we've prepared you a car at Talladega Superspeedway, a 2.66-mile tri-oval. We'll take you on a quick test run to familiarize you with your stock car's instruments and controls. You'll also learn a little about what a NASCAR stock car feels like- how it handles at 200 mph, and how it doesn't when you've finished a few laps down.

First, you'll need to know how to make simple selections from within the game. Keyboard users can scroll up or down the various menus with the up/down arrow keys. When you've highlighted the item you want, simply press the "ENTER" key.

Joystick users can move the stick forward or backward to scroll up or down through menu selections. When you've highlighted the item you want, simply press your joystick button "A."

Wheel/yoke users must use the keyboard to select items from within the menus. **If your menus are scrolling rapidly up or down under their own power, press the "J" key at the Main Menu to disable menu joystick control.** NASCAR Racing does not support mouse control, except when using the accompanying Paint Kit.

When you start NASCAR Racing, the first thing you'll see will be the Main Menu. Using the keyboard or your joystick, select Preseason Testing. This will give you an opportunity to test your stock car on a closed course, without any other drivers to worry about.

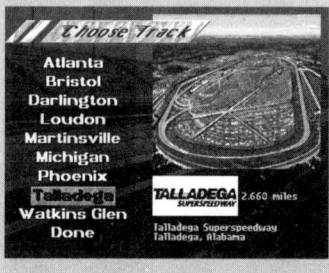

Now, choose Talladega from the Track Selection menu (if you don't see Talladega on your screen, don't panic; You may have to scroll down the list until you reach it). Talladega Superspeedway's fast, high-banked turns and wide straightaways will give you plenty of room for this session. As one driver puts it, "Mastering Talladega is about 85% car, 15% driver."

Here we are at the Preseason Testing screen. You're able to drive as many laps as you wish during test sessions. However, you will need to make pit stops for additional fuel or fresh tires as necessary. Choose Testing from the menu to head for the race track.

As you look over the cockpit of your race car, you'll notice that the driver's seat is not located in the center, but rather to the left side. This is important to remember, especially when you're knifing your way through heavy traffic. The various instruments located on the dashboard of your stock car are explained on the next page.

**Quick Start Guide And In-Car Controls**

# On Track: In The Cockpit

Your dashboard meets NASCAR race specifications. Before pulling away from the pit wall, you should take just a moment to familiarize yourself with your stock car's instruments:

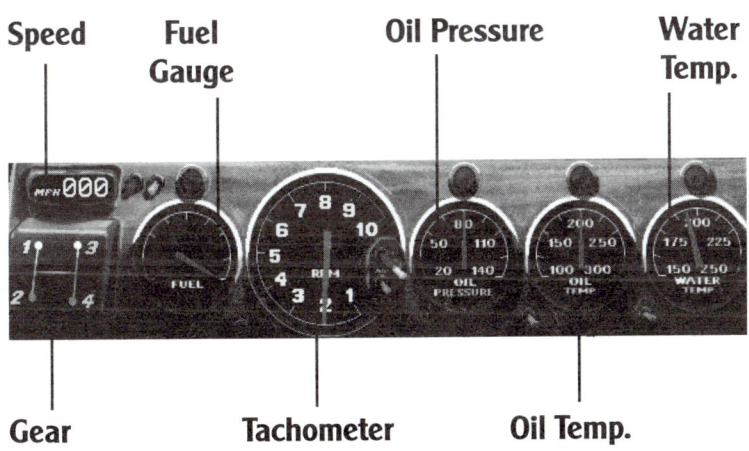

**Speed:** This digital display was created by Team Papyrus to constantly show the driver how fast the car is currently traveling.

**Fuel Gauge:** The needle indicates how much fuel your car has remaining. When it points all the way to the right, the tank is filled completely (22 U.S. Gallons). When the needle begins to touch the red area, your car has three gallons remaining. The fuel gauge has a **Red Warning Light** mounted directly above it. This light will begin to blink when you have three gallons remaining. Better head for the pits for another tankfull!

*Quick Start Guide And In-Car Controls*

**Oil Pressure:** Normal operating pressure is 80 psi. Over-revving the engine will cause the warning light above the oil pressure gauge to blink. **Continuous over-revving is a serious condition, often causing the engine to blow.** If the oil pressure light blinks constantly, pull into the garage and pick different gear ratios- otherwise your engine builder won't be very happy.

**Water Temperature:** Normal temperature is approximately 200 degrees. Like some of the other gauges, the water temperature display is equipped with a red warning light (these are often referred to as "idiot lights"). The warning light will flash if the temperature gets too hot. **Water temperature can increase under two conditions: the driver is spending too much time drafting behind other cars, robbing the radiator of its needed airflow; or, the driver is running the car too hard, perhaps over-revving the engine for extended periods of time.** The temperature of the outside air can also cause fluctuations in the water temperature. Remedy the situation during a race by slowing down or pulling into the pits for repairs. During practice or warm-up sessions, you may want to head for the garage to make a gear ratio adjustment.

**Gear:** This digital display was created by Team Papyrus to constantly show the driver what gear the transmission is currently in.

**Tachometer:** The largest dial on the dash, and perhaps the most important. This shows the driver the current engine rpm's. Watch the tachometer (also called a "tach") to shift gears at the appropriate moment. This will help prevent engine over-revving. The tachometer numbers are read in thousandths (1,000 to 10,000 rpms). **Generally, you should try to shift up when the needle reaches between 7,000**

*Quick Start Guide And In-Car Controls*

**and 8,000 rpms.** The needle points straight up (twelve o'clock) when the rpms are at 8,000. This is where most drivers want the needle to be. **Revving the engine constantly beyond 9,000 rpms could lead to engine failure.** If your oil pressure warning light blinks constantly while in fourth gear at high speed, you probably need to change gear ratios.

**Oil Temperature:** This gauge shows the driver the current temperature of the engine oil. Normal readings should be in the 200 degree range. Excessive oil temperatures will activate the red warning light above the dial. This indicates that overall, the engine is running too hot. Remedy the situation by increasing the rear spoiler angle in the pits. In practice or warm-up sessions, you may also want to adjust gear ratios.

Additionally, your car is equipped with a 3-way rear-view mirror. The left section shows traffic to the left of your car. The middle section shows traffic directly behind your car. The right section reflects traffic on your right.

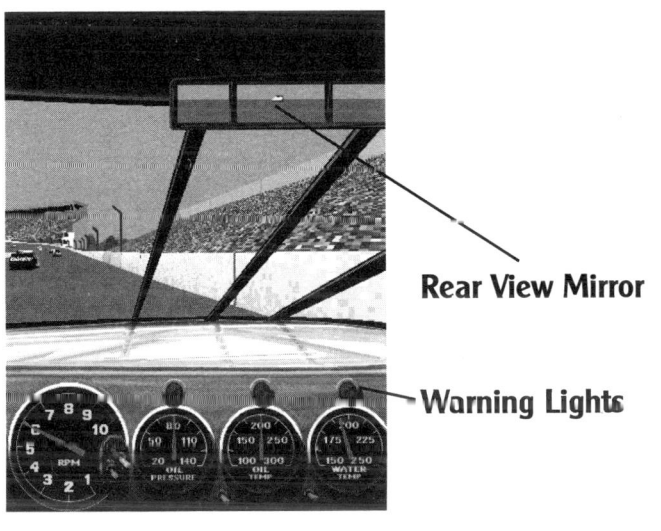

*Quick Start Guide And In-Car Controls*

Now that you've skimmed the dashboard, you're ready for some "seat" time. Slowly begin to accelerate out onto the track. Even though you'll be the only driver out there, it would be good to get into the habit of checking that rear-view mirror about now.

Unless you've already found the **"Driving Aids"** selection on the **Realism Menu** and turned off **"Automatic Shifting,"** the computer will handle the stickshift for you. If you've already selected **"Manual Shifting,"** watch that tach! Shift up at 7,000 rpms. We're up to third gear so far, and the tach shows 6,000 rpms.

Talladega's 33 degree banking, up close and personal. Try not to overcorrect the steering as the pavement pitches the car. Keep an eye on the top left corner of the windshield; you'll see what lies ahead. Incidentally, that dotted line near the outer wall is located 10 feet from the barrier.

Nearing the end of the back straight, we're in fourth gear and going pretty fast. See that orange ball to the right? There's a NASCAR official located in each of those. The balls are positioned at the start and end points of each corner. We'll try to enter turn three from just right of center. Note how all of the engine-related needles are standing almost straight up. That's a good sign that the car is setup properly.

*Quick Start Guide And In-Car Controls*

Just coming off of turn four, you'll see the pit entrance to the left. If you want another lap, stay to the right and head for the tri-oval. If you want to pit, start getting on the brakes now.

Don't be late for a date with the tri-oval! In order to go fast through there, you'll have to start high, then cut low across the apron as shown here. Again, try not to overcorrect.

As you streak across the start/finish line, you'll notice that the **Pit Board** appears in the upper left corner of the cockpit. The top line **(marked "L")** shows you the average speed of the last lap completed. The bottom line **(marked "B")** shows you the best lap average you've achieved during this session. Seems we did a 174.115 on this maiden lap.

At anytime while driving, you can press the **"ESCAPE"** key to return to the menu. On the **Preseason Testing Menu**, you'll see a clip of replay footage playing to the right. You can now select **Replay** to view more extensive coverage of your driving exploits. Choose **Garage** to "head for the shed" to do some tweaking. When you choose **Resume**, you'll be back in the car, right where you left off, or in the pits if you've visited the **Garage**. (Take note: if the car was moving when you headed for the menu, it will be moving when you **Resume**).

*Quick Start Guide And In-Car Controls*     11

# The Pit Board

The pit board appears momentarily in the upper left corner of the cockpit as you cross the start/finish line. This board gives you important results of the most recent lap driven.

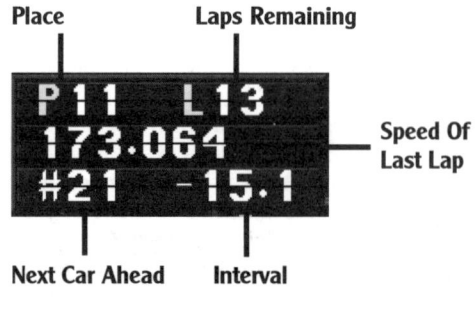

In this example, the player's car is currently in eleventh place. 13 laps remain in this race, with the last lap speed averaging 173.064 mph. The player trails car #21 by 15.1 seconds.

12　*Quick Start Guide And In-Car Controls*

# Pausing The Action

You can pause the simulation at any time by simply pressing the **Pause** key. This is the letter **"p"** on the keyboard. Aside from taking a break, the **Pause** key is useful duing radio communications. After pressing **"p"** to pause the game, use the function keys to display radio information. Use the radio to instruct your crew on the adjustments you want at the next pit stop. Press **"p"** a second time to resume the action.

Use the **"p"** key to freeze the action in progress. Press **"p"** once to pause the game; press **"p"** a second time when you're ready to continue. The **Pause** key is especially useful when operating the two-way radio. By pausing the action, you can make radio selections without the burden of driving. When you've finished using the radio, pick up right where you left off by pressing the **Pause** key a second time.

*Quick Start Guide And In-Car Controls*

# Using Your Radio

Your stock car is equipped with a two-way radio. This allows you, the driver, to stay in contact with your pit crew while you're out on the race track. You can use the radio to give your crew instructions for the next pit stop, or get current performance information about your race car. **You cannot acquire radio information while using the arcade view.**

To use the radio while driving, we recommend you first pause the game, using the **"p"** key. Next, choose any function key from F1 through F8 to display radio information. This information will appear superimposed atop the right side of the dashboard.

The next few pages show you how to use your in-car radio to gather information or give maintenance instructions to your pit crew.

*Quick Start Guide And In-Car Controls*

```
F1 - Lap Info

   #74      +12.1
   #0      147.750

      Lap 2 of 159
```

 ## Lap Info

At anytime while in the cockpit, press **"F1"** to get lap information via the radio. This screen displays your car number, most recent (last) lap average speed and the number of the lap you are currently driving. You will also see the number of the driver immediately ahead of you, along with the interval (the length of time you trail that opponent by). If you are leading the race, the opponent car number displayed will be that of the car currently in second place.

The information on the lap info screen is for display purposes only. This screen can often help give you an idea of how your car is doing throughout various segments of a race. Use the **Lap Info** key during practice sessions to learn what range of performance to expect from your race car: an average lap, compared with its very best effort

```
F2 - Standings
36 #22 B Labonte      10.6
37 #74 C Williams     10.9
38 #31 W Burton       11.3
39 #71 D Marcis       13.4
40  #0 J Tyme         21.0
```

 # Standings

While in the cockpit, press **"F2"** to view up-to-the-minute race standings. This screen shows you the position, interval, car number and name of each driver, in the current running order.

Use the **Less Than** or **Greater Than** key to "page" through the standings list, five drivers at a time. Scroll forward with the **Greater Than key (">")**. Scroll backward through the standings using the **Less Than ("<") key**. Generally, it is best to view the current standings duing yellow flag periods if you're driving. However, you can pause the game at any time to view the latest running order.

```
F3 - Fuel

Fuel: 17.7 gal
Mileage: 2.00 mpg
Proj Laps: 13
Fill To: 22 gal
```

 Fuel

From behind the wheel, press **"F3"** to display fuel information. This screen shows you (to the tenth of a gallon) how much gasoline remains in your car's tank. Current fuel **Mileage** and the **Projected Laps** left in the tank are displayed as well. On the radio screen shown above, the car has 17.7 gallons left in the tank, is currently averaging 2 miles-per-gallon and is expected to be able to complete 13 more laps before running out of fuel.

Use the **Less Than** or **Greater Than** key to tell your crew how much fuel you want them to put in the tank during your next pit stop. **If you don't bother to make a selection here, you'll always get a full tank, 22 gallons.** It is common to ask for less fuel during your final pit stop. This speeds the pit stop up and keeps the car a few pounds lighter.

*Quick Start Guide And In-Car Controls* 17

```
      F4 - Tire Temp
   O   M   I     I   M   O
  155 157 177   158 153 154
       LF            RF
  170 161 170   173 165 173
       LR            RR
```

 ## Tire Temperature

Once inside the cockpit, you can get current temperature readings from every tire on your stock car. **Inner, Middle** and **Outer** tire-edge temperatures are displayed in a "top-down" fashion.

Try to pretend you're looking straight down onto the roof of your stock car. In the upper left corner would be the **Left Front Wheel.** In the lower right corner would be the **Right Rear wheel,** and so on. The outer temperatures are located on the outer edges of the screen. When you select **"F4"** to view tire temperatures, remember to visualize the "top-down" view of your stock car for easy reading. This screen is useful to determine whether or not your crew needs to make tire adjustments to the car, based on the actual operating temperatures of its tires.

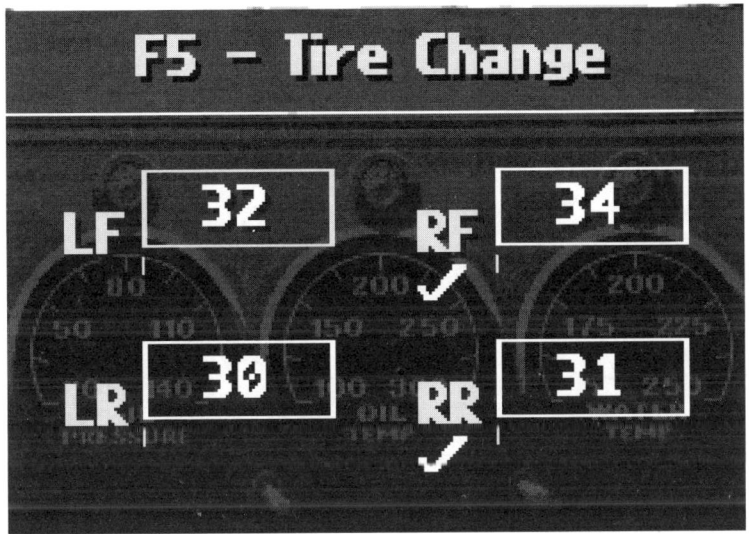

 # Tire Changes

While you're out on the track, it is helpful to radio your pit requests back to your crew. That way, they'll be ready when you come in. **Remember, if you don't tell them any different, the crew will always change all four tires and fill the gas tank when you stop in your pit stall.** But with the Tire Changes radio call, you can make specific selections regarding that next pit stop.

 First, select a tire by pressing the **"Space"** bar. Use the **Less Than** or **Greater Than** key to raise or lower the amount of pressure you'll want put in that tire at the next pit stop. A **"check mark"** appears below each tire that will be changed at the next pit stop. Press **"ENTER"** to remove the **"check mark"** from that tire. This tells the crew not to change it. Press **"ENTER"** again if you want the check mark to reappear, signaling the crew that the tire needs to be replaced. Move on to another tire by pressing the **"Space"** bar.

*Quick Start Guide And In-Car Controls* 19

 **Wedge**

You may want to tell your crew via the radio that you'll need a **Wedge (cross weight)** adjustment when you next pit. Use the **"F6"** key to forewarn your Head Wrench (Crew Chief) of this decision. If the car begins to feel *loose," adding some weight to the **Left Rear** (with the **Greater Than** key) wheel may correct the problem. Adjusting the weight at the left rear wheel also changes the weight at the right front. Likewise, adjustments made to the left rear have an affect on the right front wheel weight.

Use the **Less Than** or **Greater Than** key to select the new value for the cross weight. At your next pit stop, the crew will automatically turn the screwjacks to achieve the desired wedge. You can see the percentage of cross weight change as you press the adjustment keys.

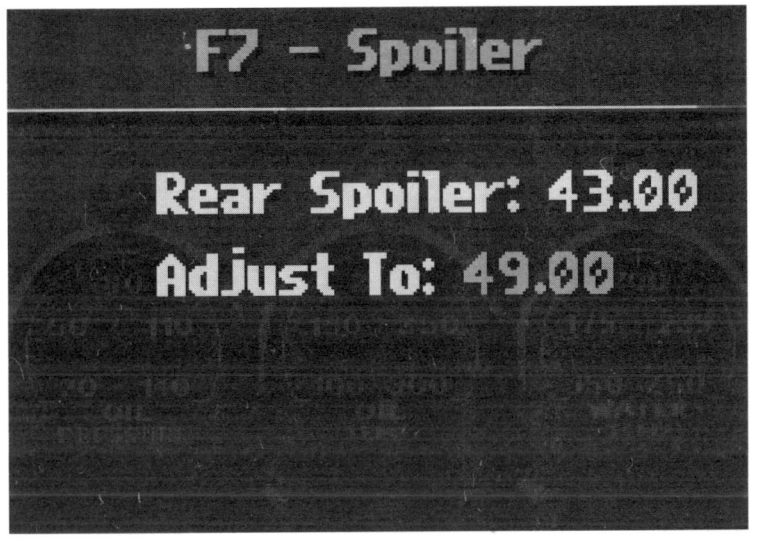

 Spoiler

Use the **"F7"** key to radio your crew of the need for a rear spoiler adjustment. Like the cross weight adjustment, changing the rear spoiler angle can correct a "loose" handling car. Unlike wedge, however, adjustments to the rear spoiler also affect drag on the car. Raising the spoiler may be a good idea if the car is too fast for some of the turns.

Use the **Less Than** or **Greater Than** key to change the rear spoiler angle. This change will then be made by your crew during the next pit stop. **Note that the front air dam is not adjustable during a race; there are too many screws that hold it into place.** If you have a safe lead, you may want to raise the rear spoiler slightly to improve the car's handling. This will slow the car somewhat, but the added responsiveness may be safer. If you find yourself trailing badly, a quick spoiler adjustment (lower) may help you reel the pack in.

*Quick Start Guide And In-Car Controls*　　21

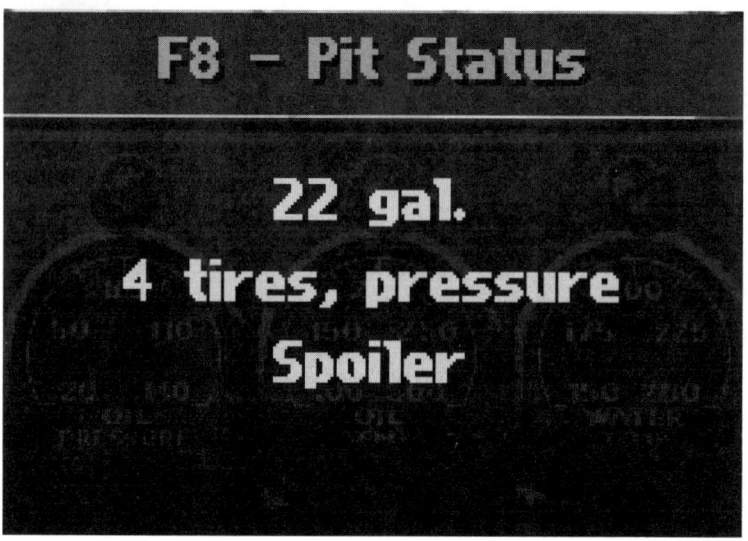

 # Pit Status

By pressing **"F8"** you can use the radio to ask your crew exactly what they're going to do during the next pit stop. This is especially useful after making numerous requests, since it's easy to forget what choices you've radioed in to the pit team.

**Remember: If you don't submit any pit requests with the two-way radio, your pit crew will always give you a full tank and four new "stickers" (new tires) when you come in.**

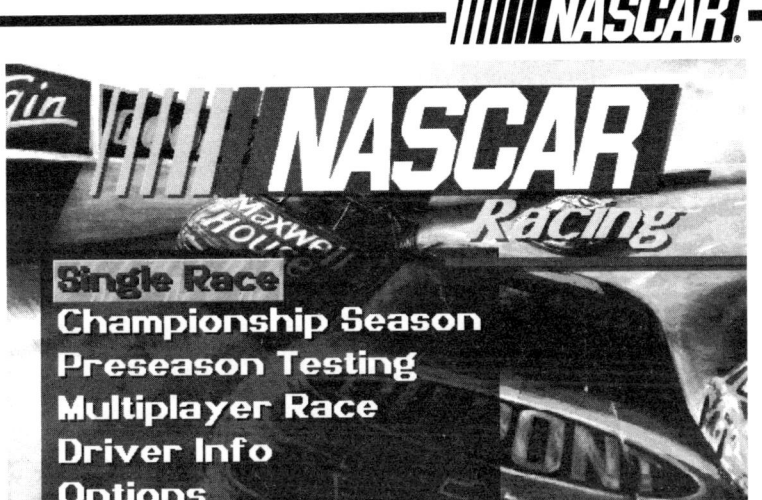

# The Main Menu

Your basic choices within NASCAR Racing are all presented on the **Main Menu.** This screen appears after the program introductions, and is readily available at other times via the "ESC" key. Each press of the "ESC" key will back you out of the simulation, one screen at a time, until you reach the **Main Menu.** You may wish to save certain items (i.e. race in progress, car setups, etc.) before exiting back to the **Main Menu.**

 You can comfortably hit the "ESCape" key at anytime while driving, without fear of messing up your race. You can resume whatever driving session you are in right where you left off, by choosing "Resume." A warning message will appear before you can leave a track, just to make sure that's what you really want to do. The "ESCape" key is a handy way to pause the action and take a breather.

*Game Menus And Functions*

The **Main Menu** selections are summarized below:

**Single Race:** Allows you to compete in a race on the track of your choice. After choosing a track, you can "trade a little paint" with other cars in practice, qualifying and race sessions.

**Championship Season:** Gives you an opportunity to vie for the Season Title of Papyrus' NASCAR Racing. Each race will be contested in order, based on the actual 1994 NASCAR schedule. This schedule will take into account only the tracks you have installed on your computer.

**Preseason Testing:** A must for every team "looking for an edge," you are provided with unlimited private test time on the track of your choice. Hone your driving skills and car setups here, without the worry of banging bumpers with other drivers.

**Multiplayer Race:** This option allows you to race against your buddies using the modem or direct connect versions of NASCAR Racing.

**Driver Info:** Ready to "hang your name over the door" of a NASCAR stock car? This selection gives you the opportunity to enter your name, pick your car make and view your opponents.

**Options:** Customize a number of game variables to suit your needs. Adjust graphics detail, realism options, joystick/wheel calibration and more.

**Exit:** Quits the game and lets you return to those boring spreadsheets, word processors, etc.

## Note To Mouse Users

**NASCAR Racing does not include mouse support.** You cannot select items from menus, drive the car or perform other tasks with the mouse. **However, the Paint Kit included with NASCAR Racing must have a mouse or pointing device.** Refer to the appropriate section in this manual to learn more about the **Paint Kit.**

## Making Selections

Use your joystick or keyboard to select items from the various menus within the game. To scroll up and down any menu, push the joystick forward or pull back; or, use the up/down arrow keys on the keyboard. To activate a selection, press button "A" on your joystick, or press "ENTER" on your keyboard. Wheel/yoke users must use the keyboard for menu selections.

Hint for joystick users: Pressing button "A" will scroll forward through certain menus, such as when you're changing cameras in replay mode, or viewing opponent cars. Use joystick button "B" to scroll backward through these items.

*Game Menus And Functions*

# The Single Race Menu

Choosing **"Single Race"** from the **Main Menu** offers you an entire race weekend's worth of action. From here you can choose to turn a few wrenches on your car in the garage, log some practice time against other drivers, or take in some replay footage. You can return to the **Single Race Menu** at any time while driving, simply by pressing "ESC." This will hold the action in place, without quitting a race. Your options contained on this menu are explained below:

**Replay:** Gives you an opportunity to view highlights from the track. You can also save, load or edit replays via this selection (See Replay section for more details).

**Garage:** Brings up the Garage Menu, where you can tinker with your race car at will. Make major decisions, save or

load existing car setups for the track you're on, or just do a little tweaking to get the kinks out.

**Practice: Preseason Testing** gives you a closed track to work with, but at some point you'll need to get used to the traffic out there. **Practice** sessions from the **Single Race Menu** give you just that, as well as a final opportunity to "shake your car down" before qualifying.

**Qualify:** When you're ready to actually enter a race, choose **Qualify**. You'll need your leanest, meanest setup on the car in order to get a fast time. You'll learn very early in your NASCAR Racing career just how important it is to start up front with the big boys.

**Warm-up:** After qualifying, load your racing setup on the car and take it for a brief spin to make sure you're comfortable with the car, track and weather conditions.

**Race:** You've done all the wrench-work, qualifying and talking. Now it's time to flex your muscle where it counts: on the track. Race distance and other variables are determined by settings made while at the **Realism Menu**.

**Next Session:** This selection lets you advance to the next session of a race weekend. For example, when you're ready to leave practice and head to qualifying, choose **Next Session**. When you are through qualifying, choose **Next Session** again to drive in the pre-race warm-up. Choose **Next Session** once more to advance to the race. You can skip any session prior to a race by simply using the **Next Session** button to step ahead. **If you bypass the qualifying session, however, you'll automatically be given a provisional starting position at the very back of the race's grid.**

**Standings:** Check the board to see where your efforts stack up. This screen gives you "up to the minute" information on you and your opposition. You can also print a hardcopy of the standings, or save them to disk.

**Saving A Race:** Anytime you leave a track before the conclusion of a race, NASCAR Racing will ask you if you'd like to save the race in progress. After saving the race, you can resume racing again anytime. The next time you select that track, the program will ask if you'd like to restore the saved race. If you choose **Yes**, the last saved race will be restored in progress.

**Done:** When you are finished racing and wish to leave the current track, choose **Done**. You will be given an opportunity to save your race or other session in progress for later resumption.

*Game Menus And Functions*

# Championship Season

Perhaps the most coveted jewel in Papyrus' NASCAR Racing is the Season Championship. This title is a testament to the overall consistency of a NASCAR team, race in and race out.

Upon selecting **Championship Season**, you'll compete on all of the NASCAR tracks installed on your system, based on their order of appearance in the NASCAR schedule. At the conclusion of each race, top drivers earn points according to finishing order. NASCAR points are awarded as follows:

| | | | |
|---|---|---|---|
| 1st | 175 | 21st | 100 |
| 2nd | 170 | 22nd | 97 |
| 3rd | 165 | 23rd | 94 |
| 4th | 160 | 24th | 91 |
| 5th | 155 | 25th | 88 |
| 6th | 150 | 26th | 85 |
| 7th | 146 | 27th | 82 |
| 8th | 142 | 28th | 79 |
| 9th | 138 | 29th | 76 |
| 10th | 134 | 30th | 73 |
| 11th | 130 | 31st | 70 |
| 12th | 127 | 32nd | 67 |
| 13th | 124 | 33rd | 64 |
| 14th | 121 | 34th | 61 |
| 15th | 118 | 35th | 58 |
| 16th | 115 | 36th | 55 |
| 17th | 112 | 37th | 52 |
| 18th | 109 | 38th | 49 |
| 19th | 106 | 39th | 46 |
| 20th | 103 | 40th | 43 |

In addition, five bonus points are awarded to each driver who leads the race for at least one lap. Another five-point bonus is issued to the one driver who leads the most laps during the race.

It's easy to see why drivers try with great tenacity to finish each race, no matter how many laps down they are or how badly damaged their car is. Though all hope of winning the race itself may be lost, it is still advantageous to finish a little higher in the standings, earning more points.

Hint: You'll visit most of the tracks twice in the same Championship Season. NASCAR drivers jot down some notes about each race weekend during the season, to have on hand for future reference.

Basic Transportation: Some of the drivers involved in this accident will be able to limp their bent machines home to the pits for some quick sheet metal work. Others may just have to stay out there in what's left, hoping it's good enough to finish with a decent number of NASCAR Winston Cup points. The rest will have to pack up and call it a day.

After choosing **Championship Season**, you'll run races in order of their appearance on the 1994 NASCAR Winston Cup schedule. This race schedule is made up of only those tracks installed on your computer.

All **Realism** factors apply to each **Championship Season**, so you should set these before the first race. For example, if you want each race to be shorter, select **Realism** from the **Options Menu** and set the **Race Length**. If, say, you choose 30% here, all races in the **Championship Season** will be that length.

**Player Info**, which includes **Tire Brands**, may be updated at anytime during the **Championship Season**. This means that you can begin a season on **Goodyear tires**, and abruptly switch to **Hoosiers** at will. (But you *did* sign that tire contract, didn't you?)

When you exit a race before its conclusion, the program will give you an opportunity to save the race in progress. During a **Championship Season**, the program will also give you a chance to save the season in progress whenever you exit the current track.

*Game Menus And Functions*  31

## Preseason Testing

Build and perfect winning car setups during **Preseason Testing.** This session allows you to drive any number of laps at the track of your choice, without the hassle of traffic.

Choose **Preseason Testing** from the **Main Menu**. Your team can then set up shop at any of the NASCAR Racing tracks. **Replay** and **Garage** functions work the same here as they do when racing. Study your driving habits by viewing **Replay** footage, then retreat to the **Garage** for adjustments. When you're ready to hit the track, choose **Testing**.

NASCAR teams do their homework. Test miles like these are run before, during and after each season to learn what the combination of car and driver is capable of.

# Multiplayer Racing

NASCAR Racing allows two players to compete against one another by choosing **Multiplayer Race** from the **Main Menu**. Each player will need a computer, with an official copy of NASCAR Racing installed on each machine. They must be connected using a null-modem cable, or between two modems running at least 9600 baud.

First, choose **Setup** from the **Multiplayer Race Menu**. This will allow you to specify or change various communication settings to suit your equipment. Set **Com Port, IRQ** and **Baud Rate** information that corresponds with your system. The **Com Port** is the serial port that your computer uses to communicate with either the modem or other player's computer. The **IRQ** is the interrupt the computer uses to communicate with. It should not be used by anything other than your modem. The **Baud Rate** is the speed which your

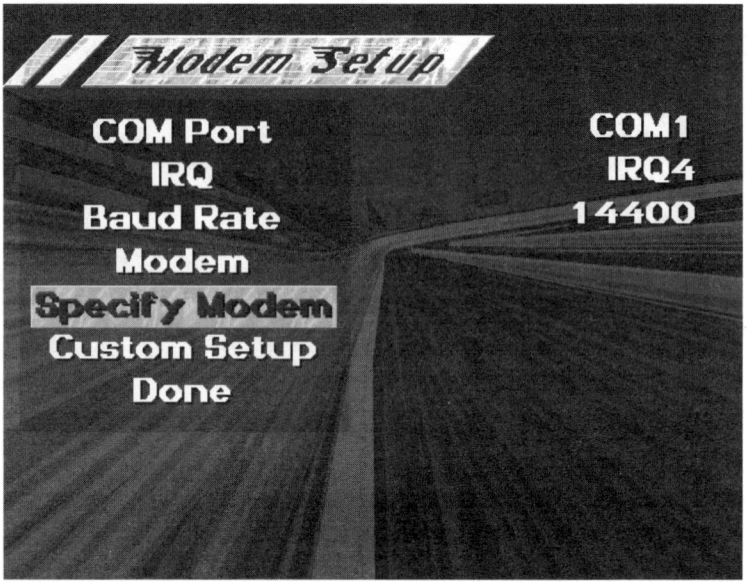

modem will operate at. **Your modem must be capable of at least 9600 Baud. When modem opponents specify two different Baud Rates, NASCAR Racing will use the slower Baud Rate automatically.**

Choose the **Modem** button to toggle between the two connection methods. **Direct Connect** will appear instead of the word **Modem** if you are using a null-modem cable.

The **Specify Modem** button opens a list of popular modems. When you choose a modem from the list, its basic setup information is loaded for you automatically.

If you don't see your modem on the provided list, you can manually input its setup information by choosing **Custom Setup**. You can also choose a modem from the **Specify Modem** list, then alter the predefined settings with **Custom Setup**.

When you choose **Custom Setup**, you have the opportunity to enter your own **Initialization String, Dial Prefix** and **Dial Suffix**. If you **Specify Modem** from the provided list, this information is taken care of for you by the program.

The most common connection problems encountered in NASCAR Racing are caused by an incorrect **Initialization String. The following features must be disabled in order to race over modems: Data Compression, Error Detection and Error Correction.** You must be sure these items are turned off, otherwise you may not be able to connect or you may experience erratic car movement. Use the **Initialization String** to disable these features. Consult your modem operator's manual to find the required modem commands. If you cannot find a listing of these commands and your modem is not on the **Specify Modem** list, please call the modem manufacturer for further assistance.

## Getting Connected

From the **Multiplayer Race Menu**, one player should choose **Dial** while the other player should select **Answer**. The dialer's machine will dial, allowing two minutes for the answerer's machine to connect with it. When the two modems connect, a phone icon will appear in the upper right corner of the screen. If the phone icon is blinking, the connection is not perfect. If the icon disappears for more than five seconds, the connection will be broken. The transmission delay indicates the one-way transmission time from computer to computer. A good connection will have a delay of 0.07 or 0.13 seconds. The longer this delay, the poorer gameplay will be (car's movements will be more erratic). The delay is caused by the phone system or by an incomplete (and incorrect) initialization string. The problem might be solved by redialing.

**Hint:** You can race against the other player without any computer drivers by setting your **Number** of **Opponents** in the **Driver Info Menu** to 1.

## Talk Mode

When connected to another computer, you may attempt to converse with the other player by pressing the **"T"** key. You should be at the **Race Weekend Menu** (which has **Replay/Garage/Next Session/Etc.** on it), driving, or watching the replay. If the other player is ready to talk, both player's names will appear in the middle of the screen, with areas above and below provided for typing. When you are finished talking, either player can press **"ESC"** to end the chat. If your opponent chooses to talk, you will see one line of that player's dialogue onscreen, to alert you of a chat.

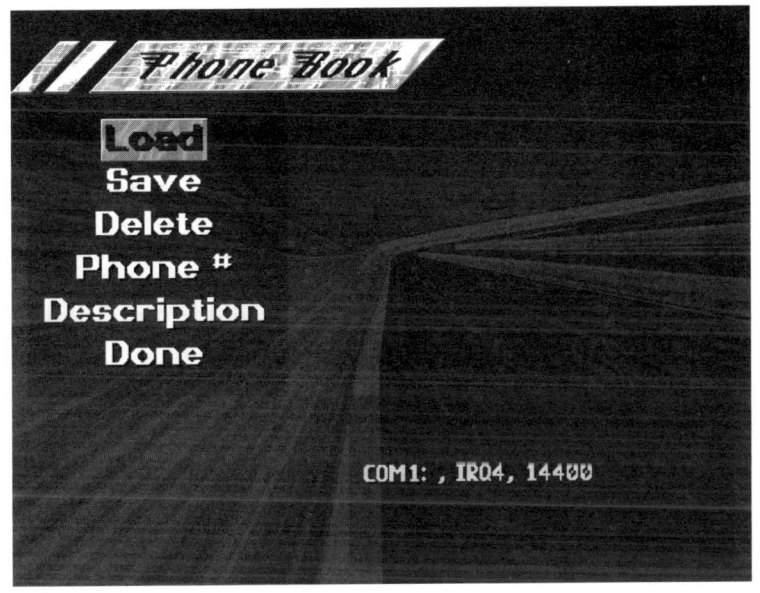

## Using The Phonebook

If you are the **Dialer**, choose **Phonebook** from the **Multiplayer Race Menu** to enter the number you'll be calling. Choose **Load** to call a previously saved number. Use the **Save** command to store the current name and phone number to your hard drive. **Delete** allows you to purge the hard drive, eliminating phone numbers that are no longer wanted.

Use the **Description** command to name or describe your current opponent. This description will appear each time this player's phone number is loaded from the hard drive.

You don't have to use the description command, but it is highly recommended. You do have to input a new phone number, or load a previously saved phone number from the hard drive before dialing. The name and phone number selected will appear in the dialogue box in the lower right.

## Troubleshooting Multiplayer Races

1. If you select **Dial** and the computer responds with "Make sure your modem is on," check to make sure the **Com Port** setting is the correct one and that your modem is turned on (internal modems will always be on).

2. If you select **Dial** and the computer responds with "Unable to initialize modem," your **Initialization String** is incorrect for your modem. Consult your modem manual or modem manufacturer for the appropriate initialization string. Make sure you have "^M" at the end of the initialization string. Also, be sure you have included three tildes ("~~~") between each command ending with "^M".

3. If when the modems connect, the transmission delay is large, this probably means that the initialization strings on one or both of the modems are incorrect.

4. If you are still unable to connect, a sanity check of the modem communications is possible using a regular communications package such as Telix, Procomm or the Window's Terminal program. Connecting via one of these packages does not guarantee that communications will work in NASCAR Racing, but if you are unable to connect in this fashion, you will be unable to connect in NASCAR Racing.

5. If both players have a DOS communications package, it should be possible to connect using that package first; then run NASCAR Racing and connect using the Direct Connect option. You must still disable advanced modem features such as data compression and error correction. This is recommended only for advanced users who are having trouble connecting within NASCAR Racing itself.

# Driver Info

From the **Main Menu**, choose **Driver Info**. Here you can enter your **Name, Nickname, Team Name** and **Hometown**. These settings all have to do with the way your name and team will be listed on **Standings, Records** and **Race Result** screens.

Select **Chassis** to decide which make your car will be. The choices are **Ford, Chevy** or **Pontiac**. The **Ford** body tends to have more downforce at the front, making it a good short track car. The **Chevy** body has more downforce at the rear, giving you a slight advantage on the superspeedways. The **Pontiac** is equally balanced between front and rear. You should know that however different the bodies are, the actual gains are minimal, based more on the driver's preference.

Select **Opponents** to view or change car data regarding the computer opponents. If you have created other car files using the Paint Kit, choose **Car Sets** to select the set of opponent cars you wish to race against.

Choose **Tires** to pick a maker: **Goodyear** or **Hoosier**.

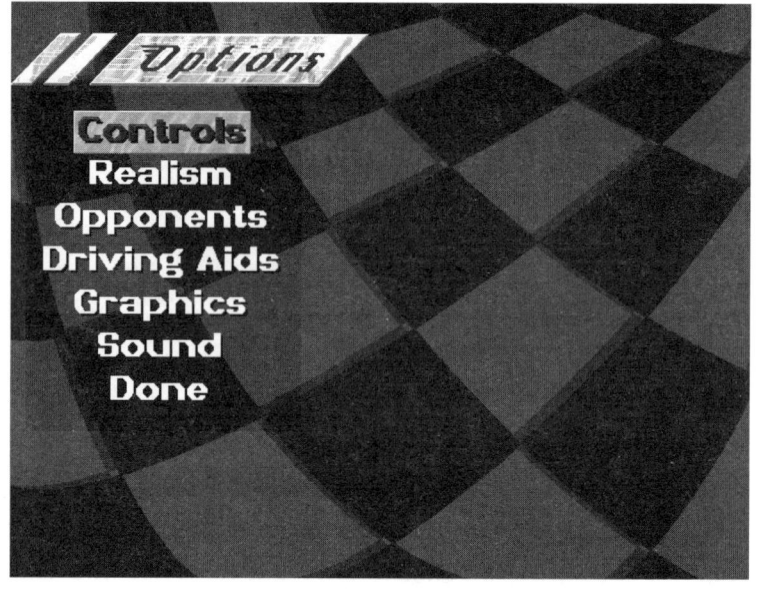

# The Options Menu

By now you've probably got a few laps under your belt from the seat of your stock car. You may wish to customize the simulation to suit your desires, and this can easily be done by choosing **"Options"** on the **Main Menu**. The **Options Menu** gives you extensive control over many of the game's features and selections, as detailed below:

**Controls:** One of the most important pieces of business to take care of in NASCAR Racing. Choosing **Controls** will unveil a menu that lets you calibrate joystick/wheel devices and decide how NASCAR Racing uses them. To do this, begin by selecting **Options** from the **Main Menu**. Choose **Controls**, then select **Set Controls** and assign each item individually. For instance, if you wish to accelerate by pushing your joystick forward, choose **Accelerate** and push your joystick forward. It's that simple! Got a steering device with pedals? Choose **Accelerate** and step on the pedal of your choice.

The screen shots to the right on this page show the menus that affect game control devices. Your selections from within these menus are automatically saved by the program, so you probably won't need to re-enter them once chosen.

**Note that wheel/yoke users will need to choose Linear Steering, while joystick owners should select Non-Linear Steering.**

Select and calibrate both joysticks if you are using a wheel/pedals device.

You can use any combination of keyboard/stick/wheel controls you wish. Note that you cannot assign keys that are already in use by the game, such as [ESC].

## Wheel Users

**If menu items scroll rapidly under their own power, press "J" at the Main Menu to disable the joystick axis during menu selections.** Wheel users must make all menu selections with the keyboard.

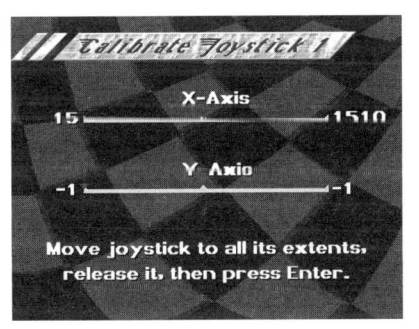

Users of conventional joysticks will need to calibrate both axes before leaving this menu. Wheel/Yoke users may only need to calibrate one axis in order to play.

*Game Menus And Functions* 41

## Realism

Decide how far inside the sport of NASCAR Racing you really want to venture. Customize race lengths, decide whether or not your car will be indestructible, allow/disallow yellow flags or pace laps to occur, and accept random weather conditions or design your own.

**Race Length:** Pick whether you want to go the full distance or just take in a short heat event. Select **Race Length** and choose **Longer** to increase, or **Shorter** to reduce the length of your race. 10% of a 500 mile race would be 50 miles. During a **Championship Season** only, all races will be contested with the same race length setting. In other words, **you cannot drive a 10% race at Darlington, then run in a 50% race at Phoenix during a Championship Season.**

**Car Damage:** This selection does not affect the computer cars, it only concerns your stock car. Choose **"On"** if you want the most realistic setting. This means your car will be subject to damage no matter what you hit. Choose **"Off"** to make your car indestructible.

**Note: Your stock car is always subject to damage caused by abuse, such as over-revving the engine or neglecting tires until they blow. The Car Damage selection only deals with the acts of hitting or being hit.**

**Yellow Flags:** Toggle the caution flags on or off. Turning them on allows realistic yellow laps at a reduced speed, while switching them off will have you driving flat out despite the wreckage.

**Pace Lap:** Turn the Pace Lap **"On"** if you want to take one pre-race warm-up lap just before the green flag waves. Select **"Off"** to begin with a "standing start," with the field lined up in order along the front straight. Pace laps are beneficial because they give you time to adjust to your surroundings while warming up your race car. If you don't use the pace lap, be prepared as soon as you enter the race track, **your opponents will start moving!**

**Weather:** Choose **Random Weather** if you want realistic, variant conditions. Choose **Constant Weather** if you want to pick the race weather yourself. Set the **Temperature**, **Wind Direction** and **Speed**. Cooler weather usually yields faster laps because the cars generate more downforce. Hotter air is less dense, robbing cars of their downforce. Hotter conditions also can cause tires to wear quicker. **Once at the track, weather will not change from session to session. Night races will automatically appear in Championship Seasons only, on appropriate tracks.**

## Opponents

Choose **Number** to change the maximum number of cars you wish to race against (using fewer cars increases animation speed on slower machines).

Choose **Strength** to adjust the skill level of your opposition (100%=realistic). This setting affects the speed other cars are capable of. If you're having trouble keeping up with the pack, lower this value to slow the other cars down a bit. If you're a real hotshoe, you may want to make things more challenging by increasing the **Strength** (speed) other cars are capable of. **Note: This setting changes the speed of all other cars on the track combined. You cannot individually raise or lower the speeds of other driver's cars.**

**Drawing** and **Heard** both concern memory issues. By pressing the **Drawing** button, you can decide how many cars in front of you can be drawn by the computer at one time, or in other words, how many cars you can see ahead of you at a given moment. Animation speeds can sometimes be slower when the computer has to draw several cars at once. If you select **Fewer Ahead**, you can reduce the number of cars that appear at a given time in front of you. This may help improve the animation speed, making it more fluid.

In general, it is a good idea to reduce the maximum number of cars drawn behind you at a given moment (seen in your rear view mirror) before reducing the maximum number of cars drawn in front. If your animation is "choppy," try reducing the number of cars behind to two or three before making changes to the number of cars ahead.

When you select **Heard**, the program gives you an opportunity to choose the maximum number of opponent motors that can be heard at a single time. As with the **Drawing** choices, more car sounds mean more memory consumed, which can slow gameplay. If your animation appears to be "choppy," try reducing the number of cars that can be played through your sound card at once. The program will allow you to hear cars that are closest to you. For example, if you select "4" with the **Heard** button, you'll hear the four cars that are closest to your car.

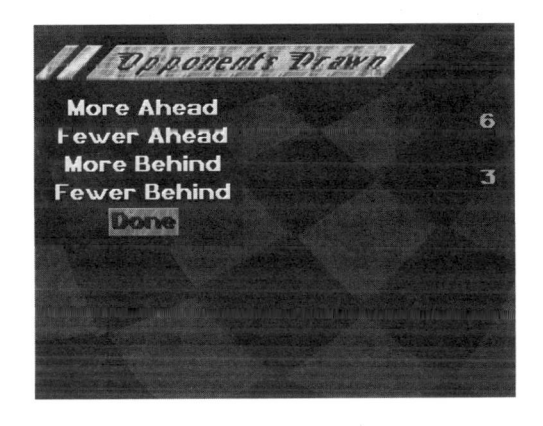

*Game Menus And Functions*

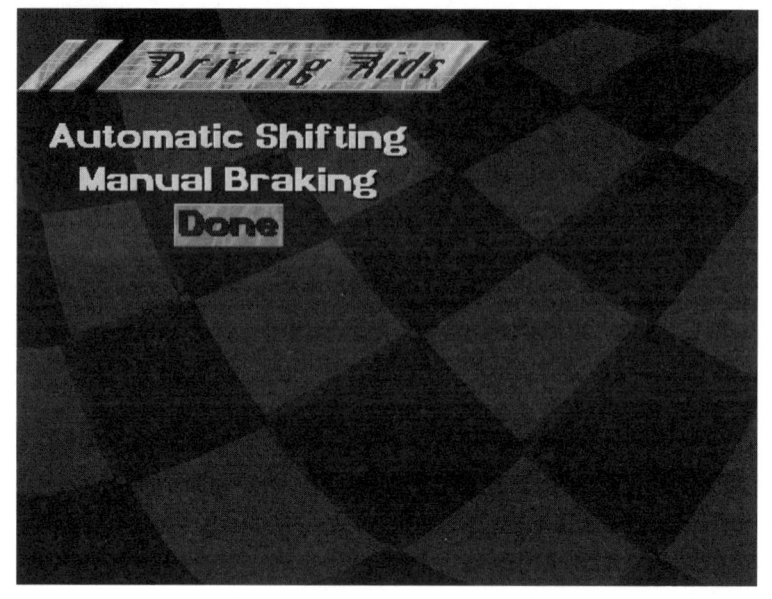

## Driving Aids

By selecting **Driving Aids** from the **Options Menu**, you can handle shifting, braking and steering duties yourself, or let the computer handle any number of these tasks for you while you polish other skills.

**Automatic Shifting** works like an automatic transmission. (Incidentally, Tim Flock is the only driver to have won a NASCAR race with an automatic transmission.)

**Automatic Braking** will cause the computer to make a reasonable attempt to slow the car as it approaches the corners.

> **Graphics**
>
> Object Textures Auto
> Grandstand Textures Auto
> Wall Texture Auto
> Horizon Texture Auto
> Car Texture On
> Smoke/Dirt Auto
> Skids/Paint Auto
> Decrease Min. Frame Rate 12
> Increase Min. Frame Rate
> Decrease Max. Frame Rate 21

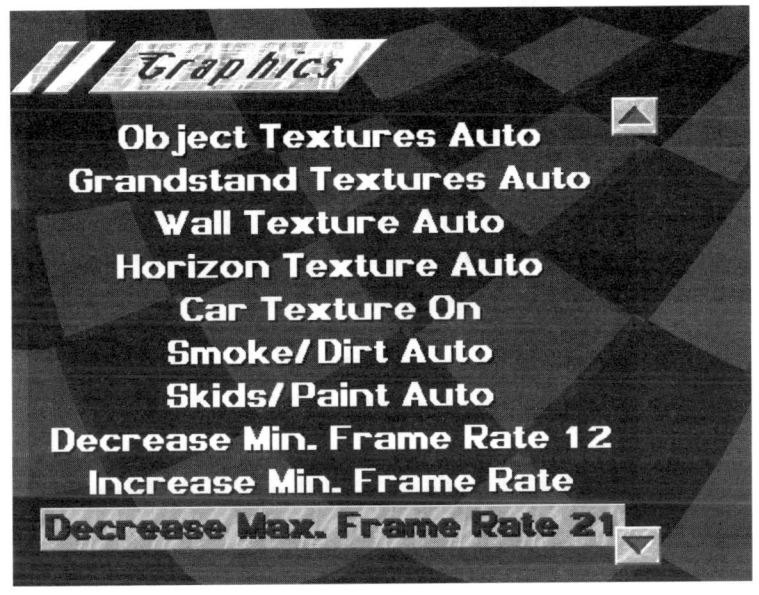

## Graphics Detail

By choosing **Graphics** from the **Options Menu**, you can adjust graphics detail to best capitalize on your computer's abilities. Each graphic item may be individually set. If the program animation seems jumpy, you may need to turn some of the items off so they will not be displayed. This will improve the frame rate of the simulation, and give you a better sense of speed and split-second timing. Turn off the graphic items that are of least importance to you, until a desirable frame rate is obtained. You may want to turn off **Grass** or **Asphalt** textures first, since they consume the most memory.

With the exception of frame rates, your choices for each graphic item are **On, Off** and **Auto**. Choose **On** if you always want to see a certain type of texture, such as the car logos. Choose **Auto** if you want the computer to adjust these items as you drive, based on how much detail your computer can handle. In **Auto** modes, textures may disappear and reappear from time to time (depending upon minimum and maximum frame rate settings), as the computer works to produce an enjoyable frame rate (animation speed).

By setting the **Minimum Frame Rate**, you're telling the computer when to begin dropping graphic detail in order to maintain smoother animation. Certain textures may disappear occasionally, in order to achieve cleaner animation. These textures will reappear based on the **Maximum Frame Rate** number.

The **Maximum Frame Rate** setting tells the computer at what animation speed to begin adding textures that were previously dropped.

**Frame Rate** settings only apply to graphic items that are set to **Auto**. Textures that are forced **On** or **Off** are not controlled by the simulation. If no texture is running in **Auto** mode, the **Frame Rate** settings are disabled.

# Graphic Hot Keys

Got a specific texture that you really want to see? Most of the graphic items can be adjusted from within the cockpit of your car by using the keyboard number keys. These keys are considered in use by the game and therefore cannot be assigned to any driving control at the **Set Controls Menu**.

The number keys and their usage is described on the next page. Each item's default setting is **Auto**.

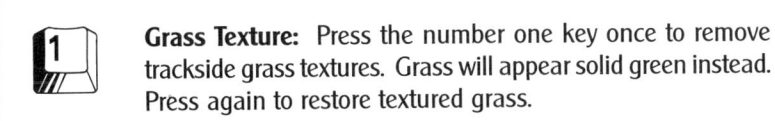

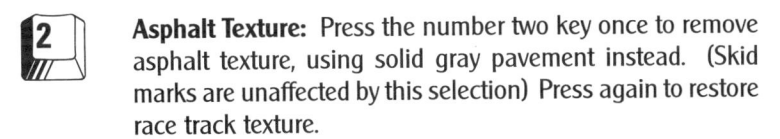

**Grass Texture:** Press the number one key once to remove trackside grass textures. Grass will appear solid green instead. Press again to restore textured grass.

**Asphalt Texture:** Press the number two key once to remove asphalt texture, using solid gray pavement instead. (Skid marks are unaffected by this selection) Press again to restore race track texture.

**Object Textures:** A Three way toggle. Press the number three key once to turn off billboard, building and some grandstand textures. Press again to remove the objects all together. Press a third time to restore all objects and their textures.

**Grandstand Textures:** Press the number four key once to remove crowd textures from grandstands. The seats will appear empty. Press again to restore crowd to grandstands.

**Wall Texture:** Press the number five key once to remove texture and signage from race track barrier walls. Solid colors will appear along the walls instead. Press again to restore wall textures and signs.

**Horizon Texture:** Press the number six key once to remove trees and other horizon detail from picture. Press once more to restore the horizon.

**Car Texture:** Press the number seven key once to remove logos and decals from all race cars. Press again to restore textured sponsor graphics to the race cars.

**Smoke/Dirt:** Press the number eight key once to turn smoke and dirt puffs off. Press again to restore smoke and dirt effects to cars that are skidding or traveling on grass.

**Skids/Paint:** Removes some of the safety striping from the track surface, as well as the skid marks that define the groove.

*Game Menus And Functions*

**Sound Levels**

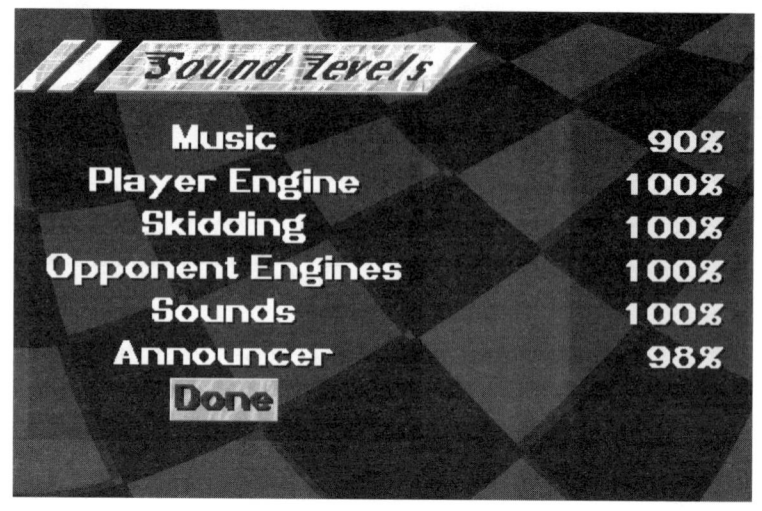

| | |
|---|---|
| Music | 90% |
| Player Engine | 100% |
| Skidding | 100% |
| Opponent Engines | 100% |
| Sounds | 100% |
| Announcer | 98% |
| Done | |

## Sound

NASCAR Racing lets you customize the symphony of stock car sounds that you'll hear within the simulation. You can turn various sound levels up or down to suit your taste. You must have a supported sound card to hear audio.

Choose **Sound** from the **Options Menu** to make adjustments. Highlight the item you wish to change, then use your joystick button or keyboard "ENTER" key to raise or lower the volume. Make sounds louder by raising the volume (100% is full volume). Make sounds lower by decreasing the volume of that item (0% turns a sound completely off).

**Note: Sound volumes can be blended with each other using the above menu. However, you may also be able to change the master volume, depending upon your hardware (some sound cards have their own volume control). Consult your manufacturer for additional instructions.**

Arcade Views: At left, the telephoto view; at right, the wide view. The information at the bottom of the screen contains your rpms, current speed and current gear. Other display items (such as water temperature, fuel gauge, etc.) cannot be seen from this view, though you do need to be aware of them. To return to the cockpit, press "F10" again.

## Arcade Driving

Any time you are in the cockpit of your stock car, you can choose to drive in Arcade Mode by pressing the "F10" key. This view provides you with an outside-rear perspective of your car, instead of from behind the wheel. Press "F10" once for the Arcade Telephoto view; press "F10" a second time to see the Arcade Wide view. A third press of the "F10" key will return you to the cockpit.

Most game controls function the same whether you are driving from inside the car, or out. At the bottom of each arcade view, you'll see some info relating to your car. The lower-left corner gives you the current tachometer reading, the bottom-center has your speed, and the lower-right displays the gear you are currently in.

*Game Menus And Functions* 51

# The Instant Replay

Replays consist of video "frames," up to thirty per second on the fastest computers. NASCAR Racing contains a powerful replay system that brings you all the action in a VCR-like interface. Each race car is equipped with onboard cameras, and is also constantly monitored by other television cameras outside the car. Instant replays can be viewed from any car upon demand. This means that when forty cars are on the track, you've got over three-hundred replay angles to choose from! Simply click to the car and camera you wish to review.

> You must be at a track to view instant replays. To access the replay functions while driving, press "ESC," then select "Replay" from the top of the menu shown. The action on the track will be suspended the moment "ESC" is pressed. Replays can only be viewed at the track they were recorded on. For instance, to view a saved replay of a race at Bristol, you must exit any other track you may be at and choose Bristol.

*Game Menus And Functions*

## The Replay Screen

After selecting **Replay** from the **Race** or **Preseason Testing Menu**, you'll see the most recent bit of footage, using the camera angle that was last chosen (TV1 is the default view). In the upper right corner, the selected camera angle is shown. In the lower right corner, you'll see a series of numbers. This is the footage counter. Each frame recorded is numbered for easy editing. In the lower left corner, the selected driver's car number and name are briefly displayed. The bottom center of the screen contains the VCR Command Bar, explained below.

## The VCR Command Bar

The heart of the replay system is the **VCR Command Bar** that appears at the bottom of the screen on any instant replay. This bar contains eight buttons that control the viewing, editing and saving of replay footage.

Simply move the joystick or left/right cursor keys from side-to side to highlight the button you wish to use, then click on it or press "ENTER." Some of the buttons also can be punched using keyboard shortcut keys in lieu of a joystick or other device. Each button is described in detail on the following pages.

*Game Menus And Functions* 53

## Memory Management

The length of available replay footage for viewing or editing is dependent upon the amount of RAM your computer has. Some tracks consume more RAM than others. Also, adding more opponents to the field consumes more RAM. Preseason Testing replays will generally be longer, because the computer is calculating the movements of a single car. The computer is always recording the most recent events that happen on the track. Footage recorded much earlier in the race will eventually be erased from memory unless you choose to save it to disk.

## The Edit Button

When saving replay footage, it is often better to conserve disk space by keeping only the segment you want. For example, you've got a replay that consists of ten laps. You want to save a spectacular crash that occurred on lap nine. You can use the **Edit Button** to remove laps one through eight, as well as lap ten. The final result: a nice, tight replay of the lap nine incident, consuming a mere one-tenth of the disk space that the unedited version would hog.

To edit a replay, cue the footage to the "in time" (the frame you wish the finished version to begin at) and press the edit button. A scissor icon appears onscreen to remind you that you are in the edit mode. Now, cue the footage to the "out time" (the last frame you want to keep) and press the edit button again. You will be prompted to save the edited version to disk.

## Select Camera  [C]

When this button is highlighted, each press of the "A" button on your joystick (or lower-case **"c"** on your keyboard) selects the next possible camera angle. Press button "B" (or upper-case **"C"** on the keyboard) to move back through the angles.

TV views simulate a racing telecast like viewers at home would see. Cameras follow your car around the track as the TV director cuts to the best angle. Some TV views also include stationary cameras, great for showing you just how fast it really is on the track. Each stock car in the simulation carries several cameras onboard, including one on each bumper, one on the roof, and even inside the car.

## Select Car  [V]

Not only does NASCAR Racing offer you a multitude of camera angles, but you can view them from any car on the track. Each press of joystick button "A" (or lower-case **"v"** on the keyboard) when the **Select Car** button is highlighted advances forward to the next car on the track. Press joystick button "B" (or upper-case **"V"** on the keyboard) to step backward through the cars.

Was there a fender-bender out there you didn't see? Use this button to zero in on the offenders. Want to know what that pass looked like from an opponent's perspective? Select their car, then choose the in-car camera angle to get a good look.

## Rewind To Beginning

This button instantly rewinds the current replay footage to the very beginning with a single press. Highlight this button and press joystick button "A" (or **"ENTER"** on the keyboard) to view the replay from the earliest frame in memory.

## Search/Rewind

To use the **Search/Rewind** key, highlight it and press joystick button "A" (or **"ENTER"** on the keyboard). Keyboard users should use the **Less Than** key as a shortcut. No matter what button is selected, pressing the **Less Than** key will automatically activate the **Search/Rewind** function. The replay will continue to shuttle backwards as long as you depress the joystick button or **Less Than** key. Short, single clicks will step the footage back one frame at a time.

## Play/Pause

If your replay tape is stopped, highlight this button and press joystick button "A" (or **"ENTER"** on the keyboard) for real-time playback. If your footage is already playing forward, pressing this button pauses the tape. You can also press the **Space** bar to start or stop the tape at any point.

*Game Menus And Functions*

## Search/Forward

This button lets you "cut to the chase." Highlight it and press button "A" on the joystick (or the **"ENTER"** key on the keyboard). As you hold your button down, the replay footage will rapidly spin forward until you release it. Quick bursts of this button will step the tape forward one frame at a time. Keyboard users will find the **Greater Than** key provides a handy shortcut. No matter what button is highlighted, pressing the **Greater Than** key immediately activates the **Search/Forward** function. Continue to press the **Greater Than** key to rapidly search forward.

## Disk Utilities Icon

Click on the **Disk Utilities** button to **Load, Save** or **Delete** replay footage. When you choose **Load**, a list of replays saved at that track will appear. Highlight the name of the replay you wish to load into memory. Once loaded, you can use the **VCR Command Bar** to view the footage. This will not affect any current races or action in progress.

When you choose **Save**, you will be asked to give your footage a name (eight characters or less). If a replay with that same name already exists, the program will ask you if you wish to overwrite the older file.

Choose **Delete** to remove previously saved replays from your hard drive. Like the **Load** command, you will be shown a list of existing replay tapes stored on your hard drive. Highlight the name of the replay you want to erase.

**OFFICIALLY LICENSED BY NASCAR**

*"You'd Better Have Some Headache Powder Handy"*

### Track Stats

Length: 1.522 Miles
Banking: 24 Degrees
Qualifying Record: 180.183 mph (30.4 secs.)
Date Set: Nov. 15, 1992
Race Avg. Record: 156.849 mph

# Atlanta Motor Speedway

Since 1960, Atlanta Motor Speedway has provided NASCAR fans with one of the best racing venues in the south. You can see the entire track from almost any position in the grandstands or infield. The track is noted for its long, arcing turns and short straights.

Atlanta Motor Speedway is actually located about 30 miles south of Atlanta in nearby Hampton, Georgia. The track hosts two NASCAR Winston Cup events each year, one in the spring, the other in the fall. Weather conditions differ sharply between the two races, adding to the difficult task of creating a strong car setup.

*The NASCAR Circuit*

At a glance, Atlanta Motor Speedway's design appears to resemble a true oval. But when you consider the fact that the turns are twice as long as the straightaways, a very different picture comes to mind.

Veteran NASCAR driver Dave Marcis explains, "Even though Atlanta is a mile-and-a-half and looks like it's got a pretty good straightaway, when we do testing there, computers show a minimum of about a half-a-g of force on the driver. This indicates that the way you drive that race track, you never really get going straight ahead. You're always in some sort of an arc, it just almost makes a complete circle the way you gotta drive it."

## Atlanta Setup

NASCAR Driver Joe Nemechek
On Preparing A Car For Atlanta:

"Atlanta is a pretty intimidating race track. You don't want the car loose, you want the thing as neutral as possible; maybe just a little bit of push, if anything. Atlanta is similar to Michigan- the driver who picks the gas up early usually has the best run off of the corner, and the fastest straightaway speed. You don't always have to drive the car way down in the corners hard to have fast laps."

**Atlanta Setup Priority List**
**by Gary Nelson**
**NASCAR Winston Cup Series Director**

Horsepower
Handling
Downforce
Drag

*The NASCAR Circuit*

**OFFICIALLY LICENSED BY NASCAR**

# Finding The Line At Atlanta

Dave Marcis has driven in more NASCAR races than any other driver, except Richard Petty. His personal list of race victories includes a win at Atlanta in 1976. Here's how Dave assesses the track:

*"Atlanta is a very fast race track for the size of it. You enter turn one quite high. As you turn in, you go down low to the apex at the middle of the corner.*

*"You let the car drift out up off of turn two. You run pretty tight up against the wall down the back straightaway.*

*"The entrance into turn three is not quite as high an entrance as some of the other race tracks. You go in there at more of an angle, and you don't really make your turn until you get toward the middle of three and four.*

*"You try and get the car, again, down low. Let the car drift out coming up off of turn four; run down the front straightaway pretty much up against the wall again."*

## "World's Fastest Half-Mile Speedway"

### Track Stats

Length: .533 Mile
Banking: 36 Degrees
Qualifying Record: 122.474 mph (15.7 secs.)
Date Set: April 5, 1992
Race Avg. Record: 101.074 mph

# Bristol International Raceway

Located just off I-81 in Northeast Tennessee, Bristol International Raceway has been offering door-to-door NASCAR Racing since 1961. The 36 degree slopes are the steepest on the circuit.

Bristol has seen its share of streaks: Cale Yarborough once won 8 out of 12 races here, while Darrell Waltrip won 7 in a row. Bristol also owns NASCAR records for most lead changes and most caution flags in a race.

**OFFICIALLY LICENSED BY NASCAR**

# Bristol Setup

After circling Bristol International Raceway in practice, you might plan on starting with as tight a car as you can build. Later, as you pick up more experience on this daunting oval, you might take a different approach to your car setup.

Start by pulling the left bias to about 1825 lbs., and the rear bias to 1700 lbs. Get the rear spoiler up all the way, and the air dam at 50% max height. Now, take a few test laps to get an idea of how the tires are doing. After checking tire temps, adjust pressures, camber and wedge (cross weight) to get the handling you need. Use only as much wheel lock as you need to take the car high or low in the corners. Excessive wheel lock at Bristol will have you testing your car's roof flaps often.

Use shorter, tighter gear ratios to produce powerful acceleration rather than top speed. Finally, make final adjustments to your rear spoiler and wedge positions to suit your driving style.

### Bristol Setup Priority List
### by Gary Nelson
### NASCAR Winston Cup Series Director

- Handling
- Horsepower
- Braking
- Downforce

# Coping With The Oval Of Madness

NASCAR Driver Joe Nemechek takes you on a tour of Bristol's banks:

*"Coming up to the start/finish line, you're right up against the wall, keeping the car as tight as you can against it. When you start getting into turn one, you can't jump off the gas, you gotta roll out of the gas. Touch the brakes, enough to just get the car slowed down a little bit. You have to make sure that the left-side tires are right down at the bottom of the white line. Just before the center of the corner, you need to be back on the gas about half-throttle. Just past the center of the corner you should be three-quarters throttle, and then three-quarters of the way through turn two you're back wide open on the gas, coming off.*

*"The car wants to push up a little bit in the middle of the corner; it kinda makes a diamond. It goes up a little bit and then you try coming back across coming off of two, right down to the bottom with the left-side tires, right against that white line. Coming off the corner there's a bump. A lot of times they'll spin the back tires just a little bit coming off of turn two at Bristol."*

**OFFICIALLY LICENSED BY NASCAR**

*"Again, right up against the wall as close as you can be. Goin' into turn three is probably the trickiest corner because the cars have a tendency to get loose into the corner. Back off the gas just before you start turning into the corner, again keeping a light brake when you go into the corner. Down to the bottom, get the left-side tires right close to the white line. The car goes up the race track a little bit; just before halfway through the corner you pick the gas up. Just after the center you're about half-throttle, and you're pickin' the throttle up as you're coming off. Again, coming off of turn four you wanna get those tires right down to the white line, because once you come past that point the race track flattens off, and it throws the car to the outside wall."*

It's never hard to find trouble at Bristol. With 30-plus cars in the tight confines of about a half-mile, 36 degree banking and slippery concrete surface, there are enough obstacles to keep your attention. Try to keep your nose clean early, let the other folks have at it instead. Later on, when some of the cars have called it a day, you'll have more room to run the line you want to. If you find yourself a lap or two down, don't worry- on a track this short, you can pick up a lap, if you get a real fast pit stop. (Papyrus Photo)

The NASCAR Circuit

*"Too Tough To Tame"*

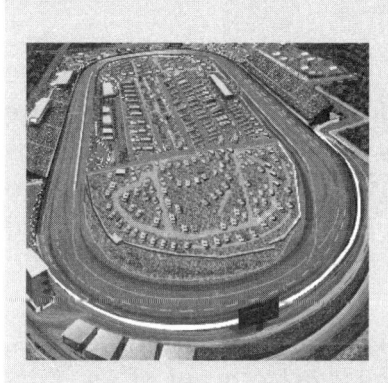

### Track Stats

Length: 1.366 Miles
Banking: 23 Degrees in turns 1&2
25 Degrees in turns 3&4
Qualifying Record: 163.067 mph (30.1 secs.)
Date Set: March 27, 1992
Race Avg. Record: 139.958 mph

# Darlington Raceway

Carved from an old cotton field on the outskirts of town, Darlington Raceway is NASCAR's oldest superspeedway. Opening in 1950, Darlington Raceway features a narrow racing groove and disproportionately banked corners. This track has always held a certain mystique among drivers, each one knowing that when they've conquered this oval, they'll have the undivided attention and admiration of their peers.

Racing successfully on this egg-shaped oval requires a well-engineered car, a little experience and lots of luck. Your skills at driving in bumper-to-bumper traffic will be severely tested, as well as your level of patience as a driver. Darlington Raceway has tripped, kicked, punched and slapped some of the biggest names in NASCAR Racing- and now it's ready to add your name to the list!

## Darlington Setup

NASCAR Driver Joe Nemechek
On Setting Up For Darlington:

*"There you need a car that's neutral, but you can stand the car to be a little bit on the loose side to go fast, because cars seem to get real tight during the race. The key there is getting through turns three and four, and knowing when to turn coming off of turn four. If you know when to turn you can hold the gas wide open and make the corner.*

*"It's hard to explain, but you really gotta watch the racetrack. Because of the banking, you can't see out of the front windshield; you're kinda lookin' right out the top corner of the windshield. There's no reference points of when to turn, you watch the black marks on the race track from where the rubber's being put down. And you have to know what your car's doing at that particular time so you know that 'when you turn' is going to compensate for whatever the car's doing."*

**Darlington Setup Priority List
by Gary Nelson
NASCAR Winston Cup Series Director**

Handling
Horsepower
Downforce
Braking
Drag

# Trying To Tame Darlington

Though Dave Marcis has never won a race at Darlington, he has had several top fives:

"Enter turn one fairly high. You definitely have to get down low before the apex. Stay low through turns one and two. You run about a car-width away from the wall up the back straightaway.

"On the entrance into turn three you'll go right on down against the apron. Let the car drift high, right up against the wall. You run through the middle of that corner tight up against the wall, and then you make a turn, kinda cuttin' straight across on an angle, and get down against the apron again for the exit of turn four.

"Darlington is very unique, a very, very tight race track. It's difficult to drive, especially off of turn four, and the entrance into turn three. It's basically the toughest race track that we run on for probably a lot of people. However, it's also a race track that if you get a good rhythm goin' on and you have the car working good, it's lots of fun to drive.

"Really, I like all the tracks we run on, especially the ones with the biggest purses."

**OFFICIALLY LICENSED BY NASCAR**

## "Two Drag Strips With Short Turns"

### Track Stats

Length: .526 Mile
Banking: 12 Degrees
Qualifying Record: 93.887 mph (20.2 secs.)
Date Set: April 23, 1993
Race Avg. Record: 79.336 mph

# Martinsville Speedway

Martinsville Speedway is located just outside of Martinsville, Virginia, near the North Carolina border. Originally built as a dirt track in 1947, Martinsville Speedway was paved in 1955. Though the short track was built before NASCAR was around, it has evolved into a modern racing mecca. It has been called the "Augusta National" of race tracks.

Because of the tight, shallow turns and short straights, virtually every car suffers some measure of body damage in a day's worth of racing. Like they say here, "brake hard, and brake often!"

## Martinsville Setup

Martinsville Speedway is a left-footed track. Drivers spend almost as much time on the brake pedal as they do the gas here. Its relatively flat surface, tight turns and short straights mean you'll have to back off the accelerator much earlier than your instincts will tell you.

Setups that feel a little "loose" will generally yield faster speeds here, because the driver can get back on the gas a beat faster. The gearing at Martinsville shouldn't be concerned with top speed, but rather acceleration. Aim for shorter, tighter gears that get you to the top of the tachometer quickly.

Drivers report bumpiness that will shake the car in the concrete sections, while the straightaways are smooth. This should tell you something about shock importance on this surface. Try not to use settings that are too stiff; opt for softer, slower rebounding shocks instead.

**Martinsville Setup Priority List**
**by Gary Nelson**
**NASCAR Winston Cup Series Director**

Handling
Braking
Horsepower

## How To Visit Martinsville

Here's a lap around Matinsville's tight confines with NASCAR Driver Joe Nemechek:

*"Come across the start/finish line, right up against the wall. Step on the brakes extremely hard, hard as you can push on 'em! Get the car slowed way down, and try gettin' the car down to the curb. Let the car roll through the first part of the corner, and about halfway through the turn you just start to pick the gas up. You should be off the brakes before you get to the center of the corner.*

*"Coming off of turn two, the cars just shoot to the outside wall, and they have a bad tendency to get real "loose" on the concrete in the corners. They want to spin the back tires and get the back end of the car slidin' sideways. A lot of guys spin out there.*

*"Back up against the wall, rpms go from 5,000 up to 9,000 by the time you let off the gas. Back on the brakes hard getting into turn three, you're trying to brake with the car going in a straight line and then lettin' off the brake as you start turning into the corner.*

*"By the center of the corner you should be off the brakes, and pickin' the gas up again in a continuous motion, going all the way to the floor. When you're comin' off the corner the car has a real tendency to roll over on the right side when you get up to the wall, and then it kinda levels back out."*

*"We're Here For A Little Northern Exposure"*

### Track Stats

Length: 2 Miles
Banking: 18 Degrees
Qualifying Record:
180.750 mph (39.8 secs.)
August 13, 1993
Race Avg. Record:
160.912 mph

# Michigan International Speedway

Michigan International Speedway is a superspeedway owned by the Penske Corporation. The track is located 70 miles southwest of Detroit in Brooklyn, Michigan.

If you're looking for NASCAR action that features three and four abreast cornering, you'll certainly find it at Michigan, or MIS as it is known to racers. The wide, D-shaped oval is banked at 18 degrees in the turns, 12 degrees down the front straight, and can get both speeds and blood pressures up into the red zone in a hurry.

# Building A Car In Michigan

NASCAR Driver Joe Nemechek
On Setting Up For Michigan:

*"You don't want your racecar being loose. You want the thing to be as neutral as possible. Actually, you're better off having just a little bit of tightness in the car; it helps you get around the corners faster. If the car's loose, you can't step on the gas pedal when you need to.*

*"You'll want to step on the gas as soon as possible; it seems like the earlier you pick the gas up, the faster you're gonna go. Here, it's not always driving in real deep that's going to make you go fast."*

Set fourth gear up so that the oil pressure light barely starts to flicker at the end of either straight. Remember, as you make adjustments to your rear spoiler, you may need to readjust fourth gear as well. Make sure the setup you develop will allow you to drive high or low on the track- the wide surface presents several options out there.

> **Michigan Setup Priority List
> by Gary Nelson
> NASCAR Winston Cup Series Director**
>
> Handling
> Horsepower
> Downforce
> Drag

# Lapping Michigan

Veteran Driver Dave Marcis has been in NASCAR as long as Michigan International Speedway has been around:

*"On the ideal line at Michigan, enter turn one pretty high. You'll work your way down to the apex of the corner, and get pretty low in the middle. Then, drift the car off of turn two out to the wall.*

*"You should run the back straightaway a little bit off of the wall, maybe a car-width or so. Down at the end of the straightaway, carry the car a little bit high again back out to the wall, and make a high entrance into turn three.*

*"Bring the car down again to the apex in the middle of the corner fairly low. Let the car drift out again to the wall coming off of turn four. Stay about a car-width off the wall down the front straightaway, down to the flagstand.*

*"Michigan is a very smooth, wide race track, with a wide pit road that has huge pit stalls. It's a desirable race track; the banking of it, at 18 degrees, I feel puts on a very good show and yet lets the cars be able to run three abreast."*

**OFFICIALLY LICENSED BY NASCAR**

*"You Need A Lotta Downforce On That Race Track..."*
   *-Driver Dave Marcis*

### Track Stats

Length: 1.058 Miles
Banking: 12 Degrees
Qualifying Record: 126.871 mph (30 secs.)
Date Set: July 9, 1993
Race Avg. Record: 105.947 mph

# New Hampshire International Speedway

One of the newer tracks in major league auto racing, New Hampshire International Speedway provides New Englanders with a fresh glimpse into the world of NASCAR Racing. Although the track is wide compared to other short ovals, fans in the grandstand along the main straight are treated to an excellent view of the backstretch, thanks to some tight corners.

Located just an hour outside of Boston, Massachusetts, NHIS showcases NASCAR Racing directly in the center of some of the largest media markets in the country.

# Preparing For Loudon, New Hampshire

NASCAR Driver Joe Nemechek
On Tweaking For New Hampshire:

*"You need real good brakes on the race car. You want a car here that's neutral to just a little bit on the loose side. You can drive real hard through the corners, so you have to have a car that turns real good in the middle of the corners. That's one of the key things about New Hampshire.*

*"The driver who picks the gas up early as he drives off the corner, and straightens out without spinning the tires is usually the one that's gonna go fast."*

You'll notice that New Hampshire's corners are banked to 12 degrees, but the straights are pretty flat. This can cause some excess chassis roll as the car gets in and out of each turn. Pay close attention to your shock settings- you may want to stiffen up the rear end a little bit.

### New Hampshire Setup Priority List
### by Gary Nelson
### NASCAR Winston Cup Series Director

- Handling
- Horsepower
- Downforce
- Braking
- Drag

**OFFICIALLY LICENSED BY NASCAR**

# Whipping Around New Hampshire

Dave Marcis doesn't have much experience at New Hampshire, but then, neither does anyone else. Still, Dave's a quick study, and with a couple of races under his belt there, here's what he's learned:

*"As you enter turn one, you kinda angle down in there, it's not really that round. About in the middle of the corner, you want to be right on down at the apron. Stay low comin' up off of two and then you pretty much have to let the car drift right out against the outside wall. In fact, it's a difficult race track to keep the car off the wall at the exit of turn two.*

*"At turn three, make your entrance near the middle of the race track, then bring the car on down to the apron. Run through the center of that corner quite low.*

*"When you start coming up off of turn four, try to free your car up by lettin' it drift right on out to the wall again. Then you'll run down the front straightaway about a car-width off the wall."*

*"If you see that Olive Garden car comin' up in your rear view mirror, let 'im through. You'll learn more by following me than you will tryin' to dodge me."*

**OFFICIALLY LICENSED BY NASCAR**

*"Better Make Sure You Got A Good Water Pump Under That Hood!"*

### Track Stats

Length: 1 Mile
Banking: 11 Degrees in turns 1&2
9 Degrees in turns 3&4
Qualifying Record: 129.482 mph (27.8 secs.)
Date Set: Oct. 29, 1993
Race Avg. Record: 105.683 mph

# Phoenix International Raceway

Set in a rich backdrop of mountainous terrain painted in desert hues, Phoenix International Raceway is a very demanding short oval. Each turn features a different banking and radius, and racing is often door-handle-to-door-handle.

Head wrenches often find themselves scratching their heads on race day, coping with the thin, dry air and temperamental climate. No matter what setup you leave the garage area with, one thing's for sure: you won't get all the way around this one flat out!

*The NASCAR Circuit*

## Adjusting To The Desert

Phoenix International Raceway poses some unique concerns to a race team. The race car must have strong acceleration, and be a little looser than normal to cope with the tight radius of turn one.

Start by getting all bias to the left of the car. Decrease the rear bias to slide more weight forward. Initially, this will create a push, but you'll deal with that in a minute. Stiffen the rear shocks a little bit more than the front. Lower the front air dam all the way, and run the rear spoiler at about 50%.

Pick gear ratios that are fairly tight, you don't want to have to downshift unless you have no other choice. Set fourth gear up so that the oil pressure light starts to flicker at the end of the front straight, as you enter turn one.

Take the car out onto the track, warm up the tires and check for looseness getting out of turn one. If the car is too tight, you can lower the rear spoiler further, raise the front air dam, or adjust wedge (decrease).

**Phoenix Setup Priority List**
**by Gary Nelson**
**NASCAR Winston Cup Series Director**

Handling
Horsepower
Downforce
Braking
Drag

# Flying Around Phoenix

NASCAR Driver Dave Marcis still wears a pair of wing tip shoes in the cockpit, preferring them to the more conventional racing soft shoes. He says that his feet used to get too hot in the racer's shoes; he discovered that the thick leather sole on the wing tips handled this heat problem nicely. He's stuck with them ever since. Here's another "tip" on warm climate driving from the veteran:

*"Enter turn one toward the middle of the race track, maybe a little bit below center. You don't really stay low on this race track between one and two, you let the car drift out, and you come very close to hitting the wall as you exit turn two up the back straightaway.*

*"You just let the car drift right on out to that wall, and then at that little dogleg that's there, you're way down low against the apron when you enter it. When you come off of there, you let the car drift right on out to the wall again to set up for the third turn.*

*"At the third turn you will run low through it, and about three-quarters of the way through that corner you'll again free your car up and let it drift out against the wall to run down the front straightaway."*

**OFFICIALLY LICENSED BY NASCAR**

## "The Fastest Way To Visit Alabama"

### Track Stats

Length: 2.66 Miles
Banking: 33 Degrees In Turns, 18 Degrees In Tri-oval
Qualifying Record: 212.809 mph (45 secs.)
Date Set: April 30, 1987
Race Avg. Record: 186.288 mph

# Talladega Superspeedway

Since 1969, Talladega Superspeedway has been known as the biggest, fastest track in NASCAR Racing. Talladega's qualifying record (212.809 mph) set by Bill Elliott represents a world record for stock car competition. Resting just off of Interstate 20, the superspeedway is within a three-hundred mile radius of twenty million people.

## Talladega Setup

NASCAR Driver Joe Nemechek
On Talladega Tuning:

*"You want a race car that's pretty neutral. Because of the drafting and aerodynamics, you need to have a neutral setup. People will be all around you here, and you can't afford to have the car get loose. You need a real strong engine...you gotta hold the thing wide open, all the way around. In race conditions, you start backing off and somebody else that can hold the gas pedal down all day long is gonna win the race."*

Talladega is known for being hard on a race car's tires, so begin your setup under the car and work your way up. Run some practice laps, check the tire temps and adjust cambers, stagger, or whatever it takes to even them out. Now drop the rear spoiler all the way, and begin bringing it back up one notch at a time, until you can drive complete laps without lifting up on the accelerator.

Set fourth gear up so that the engine light barely flickers just as you enter turn three. Recheck tire temperatures for equality, and adjust wedge until the car feels neutral.

**Talladega Setup Priority List
by Gary Nelson
NASCAR Winston Cup Series Director**

Drag
Horsepower
Handling
Downforce

## Lapping A Legend With A Legend

Expect your lap times at Talladega to fall short of the track record, thanks to the good 'ol restrictor plates. For over twenty-five years now, Dave Marcis has been a regular driver on the NASCAR circuit. He has competed in nearly fifty races at Talladega Superspeedway, notching a win there in 1976. Here's a lap around the speedway, through Dave's eyes:

"You enter turn one in the middle of the racetrack and get the car down low; you want to try and stay low through turns one and two. As long as the car is not "binding up" the lower line will give you faster laps. You're trying to make the racetrack shorter by doing that.

"Once you come off of turn two you run down the back straightaway in about the middle of the racetrack again. At the entrance into turn three, you turn the car down low; you run through three and four low.

"You let the car drift out to the wall up off of four. When you enter the tri-oval, you're pretty close to the wall. You turn away from the wall again and run down low on the racetrack, through the tri-oval, and then let the car drift out underneath the flag stand."

*"Stock cars turn right, too!"*

### Track Stats

Length: 2.454 Miles
Type: 9-Turn Road Course
Qualifying Record: 119.118 mph (1 min. 14 sec.)
Date Set: August 6, 1993
Race Avg. Record: 98.977 mph

# Watkins Glen International

Historic Watkins Glen International is located in upstate New York, fifteen miles north of Elmira. It is situated on a hill overlooking beautiful Lake Seneca, in a region painted with lush forest and vineyard acreage.

Watkins Glen held its first race in 1948 and hosted countless events, including the U.S. Grand Prix of Formula One. However, in 1981 the circuit filed for bankruptcy and shut down. In 1983, the late Jim Riesbeck, a Corning, Inc. executive, convinced the manufacturing giant to purchase the track in a partnership with the International Speedway Corporation. NASCAR action returned to the site in 1986.

## Watkins Glen Setup

NASCAR Driver Joe Nemechek
Talks Setup For The Glen:

*"Watkins Glen is very demanding of a driver. The race car needs to be neutral; it can be a little on the loose side, that'd be better than a push. You gotta be able to drive into the corners pretty hard, get the car turned, and then get after the gas. You gotta be able to do all that without spinning the back tires when you're comin' off the corners."*

Start your setup procedure with a balanced chassis (no left or rear biasing). Move the rear spoiler to its steepest angle, and the front air dam to its lowest ride height. Using one of the two long straights as a guide, set fourth gear up so that the car is just reaching its top speed as you brake for the next turn.

---

**Watkins Glen Setup Priority List
by Gary Nelson
NASCAR Winston Cup Series Director**

- Handling
- Transmission
- Brakes
- Horsepower
- Downforce
- Drag

# Finding Your Way Around The Glen

Skillfull road course driving includes knowing where all of the brake markers and turns are. Once again, we'll rely on the expertise of NASCAR vet Dave Marcis:

*"Watkins Glen is a pretty tough course. You enter turn one pretty high off the front straightaway, and bring the car right down to the apron in the apex of the corner. Immediately drift left out to the outside of the race track where the bumper strips are; you are in second-gear there."*

*"Just short of the entrance into turn two you will shift into third gear. You'll run turns two and three, what we call 'esses,' in third gear. As you come off of turn three and head for the back straightaway you'll shift into fourth gear. As you run through the inner loop on the back straightaway, downshift into second, make the entrance, again entering to the outside and drifting straight across to the inside. Turn the car hard left, second gear up outta there."*

*"After the chicane, you let the car drift out again towards the outside wall, and you turn down into the long corner. With a fairly high entrance, you bring the car again down to the apron of the race track, very low on the apex. As you're exiting that corner you let the car drift left out to the grass. You run up that back little short chute there, towards the tunnel. Kind of cross over to the right, and you'd be to your far right when you cross the tunnel. Downshift into second gear again to make the left-hander, run second gear across that little short chute, and then at the right hand turn onto the front straightaway just before the bridge you would shift back into third gear."*

# On The Track: Preparing To Win

*"We've done so much, with so little, for so long that now, we feel we can do anything with nothing!"*
                    -Driver Dave Marcis

A lot of Monday morning quarterbacks would love to climb behind the wheel of a NASCAR stock car, competing at the top level with no experience whatsoever. But, if you've tried to drive your stock car around the corners of Bristol International Raceway or Watkins Glen International, you know there's a lot more to taking home the trophy than meets the eye.

Actually, a lot of brainwork churns inside every NASCAR cockpit during a race. Patient driving, knowing when to brake, when to draft, and when to stand your ground like a poker player in 'Vegas are some of the skills that can only become second nature by logging mile-after-mile in practice. And, as you'll soon see- your favorite driver only makes it look easy on Sunday. In reality, they've studied their cars and these tracks in their sleep!

## Understeer ("Push")

Circling the track at Loudon, New Hampshire, your stock car just doesn't seem to be able to stay low in the groove of each corner. Instead, it tends to drift high near the wall, and it feels as if the car just can't turn sharply enough. This condition is known as an understeer or "push."

Actually, an understeering condition is caused by the front wheels losing grip with the pavement before the rear wheels do. When the driver tries to turn the front wheels, the car simply continues straight ahead, the front tires not biting into the asphalt. Several factors can create understeer: you may be attempting to drive too fast around that corner, or you may need to get more downforce to the front of the car. Shock and weight adjustments may also be necessary (see Garage section) to correct the problem if it's too severe.

**Driving Tips And Strategies**

## Oversteer ("Loose")

Again, rounding the turns at New Hampshire International Speedway, your cars rear end suddenly swings around. You fight hard to straighten out the fishtailing car, and you think to yourself, "Am I going to have to put up with this all day?" This condition is known as an oversteer. An oversteering car is said to be "loose."

An oversteer occurs when the rear wheels lose grip before the front wheels. Power supplied to the rear wheels by the drivetrain is wasted as the tires slip, looking for something to bite into. Factors that can create an oversteer include: having too little downforce at the rear of the car, excessively worn tires, and driving a car with the steering lock set too high. Other factors include shock and weight settings (consult the Garage section for remedies).

# The Racing Line

Every track has some sort of a racing line, or "groove." This is the path on the track that all of the drivers generally prefer. The racing line is usually easily spotted by the blackened rubber markings on the asphalt. On actual tracks, as more cars continue to stay in this "groove" more rubber is put down by the tires, making the racing line more distinct.

Until you're comfortable with a particular track, it is a good idea to follow the racing line as much as possible. Later, when you've found a good setup and know what your car is capable of, you might want to drive a racing line of your own.

We asked NASCAR Driver Joe Nemechek how he finds the line at a new track:

*"First, I'll watch a lot of tapes of the past races on that track, before I go out there. I'll see what the race cars are doing. When I get there, I'll go out in a rental car and run around the race track a little bit to find my line. Once practice starts I'll watch drivers, then go out and follow some of the faster ones and see if I can figure out what they're doing."*

As you can see, NASCAR drivers don't play around when it comes to finding a good groove on the track. A better racing line means better lap times, and less wear and tear on your stock car. One final note: the racing line isn't necessarily the same at the end of a race as it was at the beginning. The line your car runs best on could (and probably will) change throughout a race, depending upon weather conditions, body damage, fuel consumption and tire wear. You'll have to adjust to these changes as you drive.

## Cornering The Speedways

With a good setup, you can usually get around the bigger tracks without lifting off the gas. Because of the steep banking and shallower angles of these turns, you'll also have the luxury of several available racing lines to take advantage of. Most approaches seem to favor taking the car into the turn at the center of the track, cutting down low to the apron at the apex, and then exiting up high near the wall. **Turns banked steeper than 28 degrees generally require a minimum speed of 70 mph in order for the car to maintain adhesion.**

Short track speedways are a different ballgame, entirely. Braking is almost always a necessity, even on an empty track. On the short tracks, the driver that wins is usually the one who can be the *last one* to step on the brakes going into a turn, and the *first one* to step on the gas coming out. Since most passing will occur in the turns, it would be helpful to follow some of your opponents around the track during practice sessions. learning their styles and tactics.

Try to find a visual marker on each turn of each track, a sign, building or object that you can use to help gauge when to brake.

Road course driving demands a different style. Set the car up on the outside of each turn, and try to dive across the apex. Road circuits demand shifting, so it is essential to know what gear you've got to be in at each point on the race track.

## Bumping, Drafting, And Getting Their Attention

Drafting is a phenomenon that occurs at speeds of 70 mph or greater. It is the art of closely following other cars around the track, allowing them to break the wind for you. The end result is that your car can travel faster, and it consumes less fuel in doing so.

Constant drafting can raise your engine's temperatures by depriving the front grill of your car its needed airflow. Drafting for extended periods of time may also affect your tire temperatures, causing reduced tire life.

Drafting is a very useful tactic to employ when passing other cars. By using the draft, you can allow the car ahead to "pull" you quickly up behind it. As you get bumper-to-bumper with your opponent, dart around on either side for the pass.

By using the Bump-Draft technique, you can speed you and your opponent up a little. As you approach the other driver's rear bumper in the draft, give that car a tap with your front end. This will speed your opponent's car up; you can stay right behind, continuing to draft at the higher speed. In other words, the draft speeds you up, the tap speeds your opponent up. Be advised that this can be hard on a radiator during a 500-miler.

No matter which drafting style becomes your trademark, be patient. Set the draft up by carefully following your opponent's line. When you get "hooked up" (start drafting), look for a good place to pass, like a long straightaway. If you see none, give 'im the old tap action instead.

# Pitting

Your pit stall is randomly selected by the computer, prior to each race. You may be at the first stall one race, and the farthest stall the next. On some short track ovals, pit lanes are located on both front and back straights, with half of the field pitting on either side. Make sure you learn during practice exactly where your pit crew is situated.

Here's the proper green flag pit sequence, as NASCAR Driver Joe Nemechek relates it: "When you're gettin' ready to come into the pits, you feel good because you're gonna get new tires, and new tires mean so much in today's racing. Puttin' a set of "stickers" on during a pit stop means you'll really be able to go hard when you come out onto the track."

*"When you're comin' off the racetrack, you're right on the edge because you're going as fast as you can to get to pit road, and then boom! All of a sudden, you have to slow down to pit road speed.*

*"When you get into the pits, they change tires and give you a drink of water; but you have to be very ready. When you feel that jack comin' down after they've changed the left-side tires, you're poppin' the clutch and takin' off down pit road."*

Papyrus' NASCAR Racing enforces 55-mph pit road speeds in the simulation. Regardless, it is wise to slow down, as cars are darting in and out of pit stalls with regularity. You often can't tell if that driver ahead of you on pit road is coming (braking) or going (accelerating).

Driver Elton Sawyer brings the car into the pit stall for a quick visit. The mechanics on the car's right will change the tires on that side, then sprint to the other side of the car for a left-side tire change. The crew member at the far right muscles the two gravity-fed gas cans, weighing 85 lbs. each, while the man at the decklid is catching the overflowed gas in a canister. All of this is completed in about 20 seconds. (Courtesy of Campbell & Co.)

**Driving Tips And Strategies**

## Damage Control

Under the **Realism Menu**, you can select **Car Damage** and choose **On**. This creates some realistic accident effects. When your car suffers body damage as a result of a crash, the aerodynamics of your car are changed. These changes are more pronounced on superspeedways than on shorter tracks, though the loss of handling will affect you anywhere. Usually, your car will run a little slower because of the added drag created by the bent bodywork. In addition, your car may not get enough downforce in areas that it is needed. For example, if your rear decklid gets torn up, you won't have a rear spoiler that operates properly, if at all. The result could be that your car suddenly gets extremely loose.

These aerodynamic changes can also cause the car's engine to overheat, due to a lack of ventilation or too much drag. Overall, body damage can make your car perform unpredictably. Your crew will attempt to repair the car during the next pit stop following a crash. This could lengthen the pit stop, but it is often wise to go ahead and make an unscheduled stop to give the crew a chance to pull out the dents.

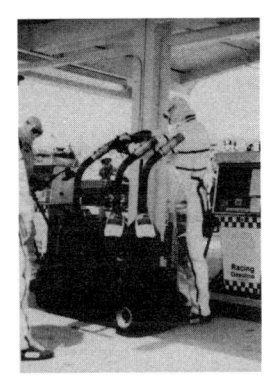

On the left, members of the refueling crew prepare the canisters before the race. On the right, Ted Musgrave's Ford gets a final engine checkup. (Papyrus Photos)

## Coping With Changes

While circling the track during caution periods, your tires tend to cool off. This causes your car to possess less tire grip for the restart. In addition, your car isn't able to generate as much downforce at the slower caution lap speeds. When the wreckage gets cleared up and the green flag flies again, it is a good idea to take it a little easier on that first lap or so, until your tires again reach peak operating temperatures. Some drivers like to weave from side-to-side during cautions, to keep the tires warm. We recommend you try this only after becoming proficient behind the wheel.

As your stock car's fuel load is reduced, the car will tend to "push." However, as your tires wear down, the car will become "looser." With a well-setup car, these two changes will offset one another, and the car will feel pretty much the same through a four-tire stop. You are likely to feel a handling difference if the team installs tires only, or refuels the tank only.

*Driving Tips And Strategies*

# The Garage Menu

Having a fast car, that's one thing. Finding a setup that fits your driving style and allows you to go fast, that's another. It's doubtful that your NASCAR race car will meet both of these criteria "right off the truck." However, NASCAR Racing gives you the opportunity to roll your stock car into your team's private garage and create a winning setup to tackle the current track.

The **Garage Menu** is available during every driving session except Race. Select **"Garage"** from the **Race** or **Preseason Testing Menus** to begin making car adjustments. The choices on the **Garage Menu** are as follows:

**Tires:** Allows you to replace worn tires, read tire temps, adjust stagger and tire pressures.

*In The Garage: Tune Ups And Bench Racing*

**Fuel:** Select "to the gallon" how much fuel you wish to carry, from 1 to 22 U.S. gallons.

**Spoilers:** Raise or lower the front air dam, and adjust the spoiler angle on the rear deck lid to provide varying degrees of downforce and drag.

**Suspension:** Often overlooked, these adjustments are some of the most critical. Adjust front tire camber, shock stiffness, cross weight, steering lock and more.

**Gears:** Fine-tune gear ratios to provide maximum horsepower where you need it most.

**Options:** Save your favorite setups, as often as you like, to disk. Got a favorite setup for this track, already tweaked and saved? Load 'er in from disk and start there.

**Done:** When you're ready to hit the track, select **Done** to leave the Garage.

## Did You Know...

The hood, roof and decklid are the only factory pieces on a stock car. Everything else is built or bought by the race team. The body of a stock car must meet the shape and standards of the actual model, and NASCAR inspectors use templates to check for accuracy in this area. The cars have a two piece rear spoiler, with a small gap between the two strips in order to accommodate the template.

# Stock Car Tires

Like most passenger vehicles today, your stock car uses radial tires. A radial tire has steel belts inside it, wound in a circular pattern around the sidewalls and tire surface. Older bias-ply designs have noticeably sharp corners instead, because they are wound in a criss-cross fashion. Radial tires have been proven to be much safer and more stable than their bias-ply counterparts.

**Passenger Car Tire Profiles**

BIAS-PLY      RADIAL

NASCAR-spec radial tires are stiff, strong, and feature a tubeless inner liner for safety. When you blow a tire, the remains are likely to stay on the rim long enough to get you to the pits.

Before you make adjustments to your factory-provided racing tires, you should become familiar with a little bit of racing terminology that relates to them:

**Contact Patch:** A term used to describe how much tread or tire surface is actually touching the pavement. In general, the bigger the contact patch you can produce, the better the grip.

**Footprint:** Same as "contact patch."

**Stagger:** Using bigger tires on one side of the car than on the other.

# Choosing Tire Brands

From the **Main Menu**, select **Driver Info**. Choose **Player** to customize your name, team and car variables. **Tires** allows you to decide which rubber factory you'll team up with. You may pick either brand, but remember: switching brands at will is a no-no. In **Single Race** events, the tire you qualify on is the tire you'll race on. In a **Championship Season**, the tire you start the season with is the same brand you'll finish it with.

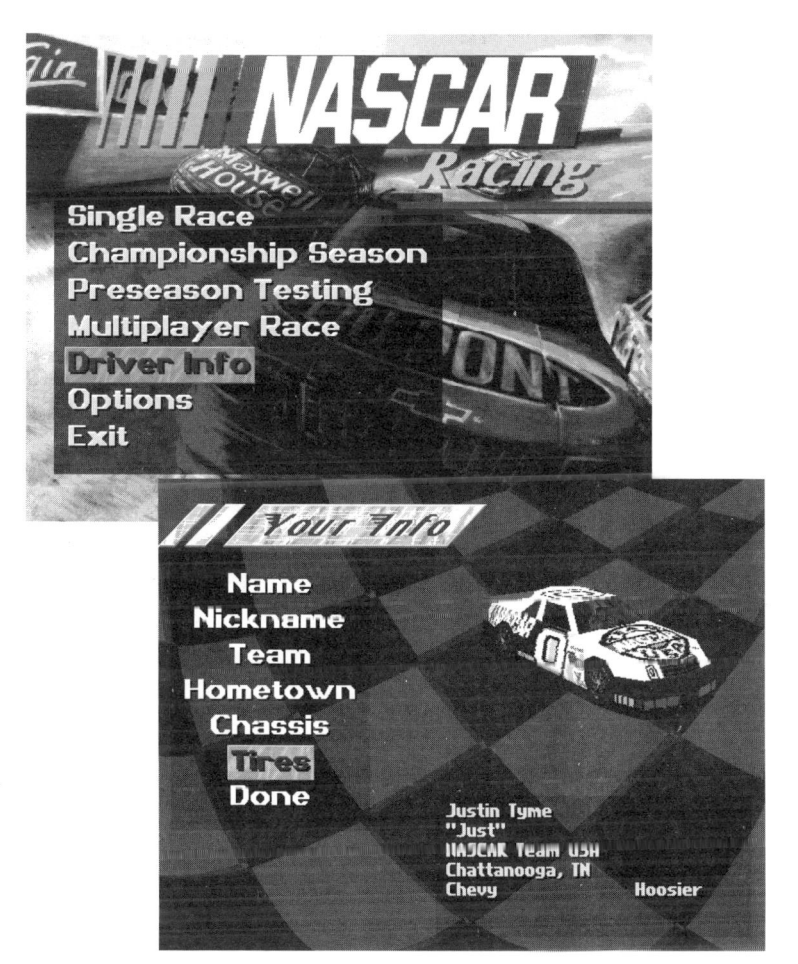

*In The Garage: Tune Ups And Bench Racing*

## Tire Compounds

Harder rubber compounds provide less grip but are more durable. Softer, stickier tires offer better adhesion but don't last as long. In NASCAR Racing, compound selection is the responsibility of the tire maker, not the race teams. Rest assured that prior to each race weekend, you'll be provided with the most appropriate compounds for the track and conditions at hand. If your tires wear out too quickly, you'll need to correct your car setup to reduce tire stress. If tire problems plague your team all season long, you may want to try the other brand at year's end.

There is no such thing has having too many tires. Each of these tires belong to a specific set, labeled and organized in order of useage. Tires that are used, but still have some miles left in them are called "scuffs." (Papyrus Photo)

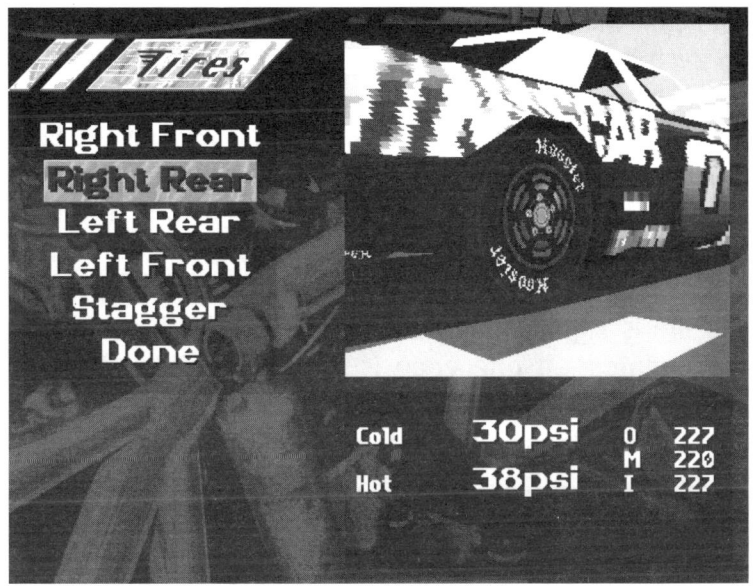

## Tire Temperatures

As your stock car's tires undergo stress on the track, they get warmer. Each racing tire is designed to operate best when maintaining two-hundred twenty-five degrees Fahrenheit. If you demand more from your tires than they're capable of, they tend to overheat and deteriorate quicker.

So, Is heat a bad thing to a tire? Absolutely not! Your tires need to reach proper operating temperatures in order to achieve optimum grip. That's why your car will handle better after a few warm-up laps than it will from a cold start. Keep an eye on overall tire temperatures as you devise car setups at each track. If a tire's average temperature is below two-hundred degrees it's probably not working hard enough. If a tire is running at over two-hundred fifty degrees, you can expect to experience shortened tire life at that wheel.

*In The Garage: Tune Ups And Bench Racing*

Your crew will obtain temperatures from three different points on each tire's surface. They will provide you with readings taken from the inner, middle and outer sections of your tires. These temperatures will indicate how evenly the tires are being worn. As a rule of thumb you'll want these figures to match closely all across each tire. This means your tires are providing maximum grip to the chassis when driven.

If a tire is significantly hotter in the middle, it's probably over-inflated. If one edge is yielding particularly high readings, suspension adjustments must be made to correct the problem. These adjustments might include or be limited to camber, ballast, wedge or springs, in that order. Remember: Shoot for two-hundred twenty-five degrees all across each tire. Do that, and you may save yourself a tire stop or two during the race.

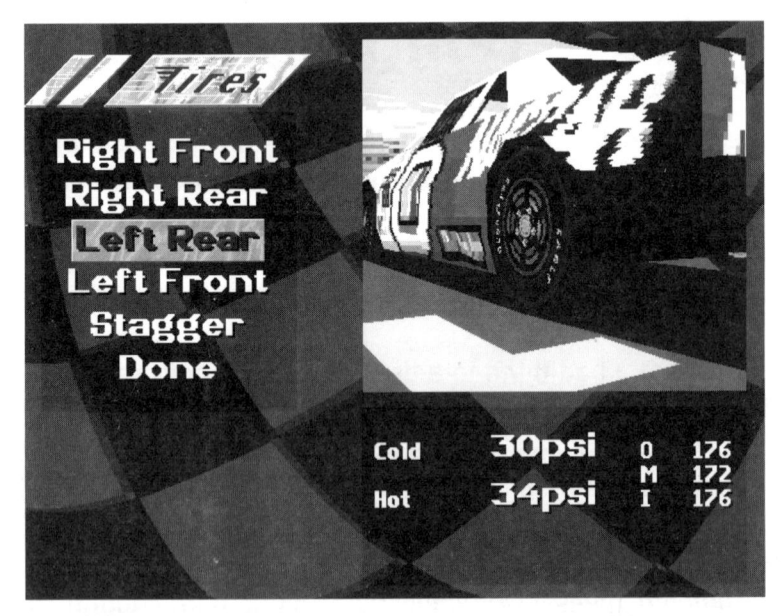

Choose a tire from the menu to see its cold and hot pressures. The shot above was taken after a 5-lap tire test at Talladega. Our car's left rear tire is 176 degrees on the outer and inner edges, while at 172 in the middle.

**In The Garage: Tune Ups And Bench Racing**

# Tire Pressures

When Milt Marion won the first stock car race on Daytona Beach in 1936, he probably gave little thought to the pressure in his tires. However, technology has marched forward and tire inflation has become a science.

Your racing tires are filled with nitrogen instead of compressed air. As your tires log miles on the track, they heat up, expand, and rise in pressure. Air is 78.06% nitrogen, but its humidity changes with the weather. The changing humidity would make it difficult for your tire man to fill the tires accurately. Yes, he could put thirty pounds in a tire but who knows what the pressure would read after eight or ten laps? Nitrogen, on the other hand, is relatively inert (inactive) and remains dry. The result: your crewman puts thirty pounds in a tire and knows almost exactly what pressure the tire will contain after those eight or ten laps.

## Proper Inflation Techniques

Correct tire pressures are essential to achieve prolonged tire life and maximum gripping power. A tire that is over-inflated will be hotter in the center, while an under-inflated tire will be hotter on its outer edges.

(Papyrus Photo)

A tire's "profile" can be changed drastically by inflating to various levels. An under-inflated tire will sag in the middle, while an over-inflated tire will protrude in the center. These changes

*In The Garage: Tune Ups And Bench Racing*　　103

in profile affect the rolling drag of that tire. An under-inflated tire will tend to be more flexible, provide better grip and increase in temperature- but at a price of reduced speed because of the additional rolling drag.

What is the right pressure to run with in your tires? Start by running a few laps at race speed and noting the temperatures at each wheel. In the screen shot at left, the chosen tire is 4-degrees cooler in the center than it is at the edges. By adding a slight amount of pressure, another test run may produce even temperatures all across the tire. This will generally result in the longest tire life.

| | | | |
|---|---|---|---|
| Cold | 30psi | O | 176 |
| | | M | 172 |
| Hot | 34psi | I | 176 |

If you have trouble getting a tire hot enough to provide some sticking power (about 200-degrees), you can deliberately run the pressure a little on the low side. This may increase the wear and tear on that tire, but you may pick up an extra bit of needed traction.

## Cold & Hot Pressures

When you select a tire from the Tires menu, you will receive two pressure values from that tire. Cold pressure shows you what the tire is originally filled to, before it's run. Hot pressure gives you a current pressure reading of the tire. This information gives you an idea of how much pressure is building in each wheel.

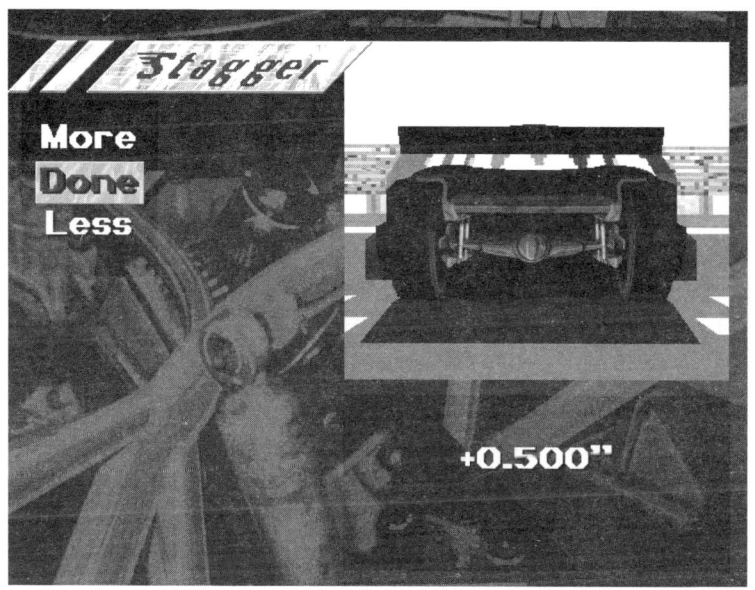

# Wheel Stagger

Although many American sedan models feature front-wheel drive technology, a NASCAR stock car employs a conventional rear-wheel drive scheme. This means the engine directly powers the rear wheels (also called the "drive wheels") via a driveshaft and differential assembly. The engine turns the drive shaft, which rotates the rear wheels. The NASCAR differential is called a "Detroit Locker," a limited slip differential which keeps either drive wheel from spinning faster than the other under power. It locks under power, unlocks under trailing throttle (drafting) or braking. **Wheel Stagger** is effective while the differential is locked.

Wheel stagger is a term used to discribe the relationship of tire diameters between the right and left side tires. Race teams will often use larger tires on the right side of the car because it is the outer side of the car on NASCAR ovals. By using positive wheel stagger (using larger circumferences on the right side) your car may be easier to drive in the turns. The positive stagger may also cause the car to pull to the left on straightaways.

Before radial tires came to NASCAR, teams would often adjust wheel stagger by inflating the tires to different levels. The additional air would expand the tires vertically. The left side may have carried thirty pounds in each tire, while the right side carried forty-five. But additional pressure inside a radial tire causes lateral expansion, not vertical. So, the manufacturers create racing tires in a variety of diameter sizes for your team.

You will almost always want some positive stagger on oval courses, while using little or no stagger on road circuits. Additionally, you'll want larger amounts of stagger on the shorter tracks, because on tighter corners, the outside wheel travels further, relative to the outside wheel.. The abbreviated straights also give your race car less time to build top speed coming out of the turns, so you'll want to maintain as much speed in the corners as possible.

## Tire Summary

**Tire Types:** Goodyear more durable, Hoosier stickier.

**Temperatures:** Even temps all across each tire generally provide best grip.

**Lower Pressure (Middle Temp Too Low):** Causes the tire surface to "sag," creating more rolling drag and making the tire run hotter. This can be desirable if you're looking for more grip.

**Optimum Pressure (Even Temps):** After warmup, if inner, middle and outer temps match, maximum tire life can be expected.

**Higher Pressure (Middle Temp Too High):** Causes the tire surface to "crown," slightly increasing the shock rates and making the tire run cooler. This may be desirable if you want a firm, fast tire with less grip.

**Stagger Pros:** Can improve car's grip in corners.

**Stagger Cons:** Can pull the car to the left on straights.

**Note:** The summary above only considers the tire menus and their effects. Many other factors affect a tire's readings and consistency. They are: **Weight Jacking, Shock Stiffness, Track Temperature, Camber, Downforce, Speed** and yes, even **Driving Style.** Consult the sections about other **Garage Menu** items for information on how to adjust them.

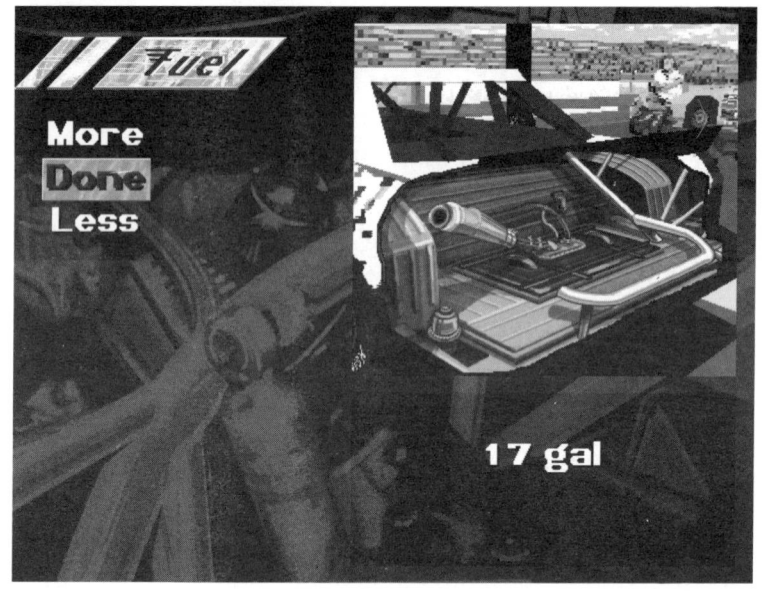

## Fuel

Your race car burns unleaded gasoline, but you can't buy this stuff at the corner Dixie Mart. Over-the-counter hi-test is 93-octane, but your stock car's fuel has an octane rating of well over 104!

In a nutshell, octane ratings indicate the fuel's ability to resist premature detonation and burn evenly inside an engine. The higher the octane number, the more anti-knock additives found in the gasoline.

## Fuel Storage

Fuel is stored onboard your race car directly behind the rear axle. The tank itself has a 22-gallon capacity and includes a "bladder" (a rubberized sack that houses the gasoline) to prevent fuel spillage during a crash. About 1% of this bladder is filled with a highly absorbent foam material; the foam soaks the gasoline up much like a sponge. This stabilizes the fuel and prevents it from sloshing back and forth inside the tank.

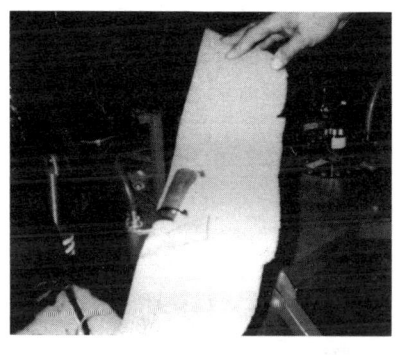

Shot depicting foam material that fills the fuel cell. The foam stabilizes the fuel supply so that it can't jeopardize the car's handling. (Vandergriff Photo)

It is important to note that each gallon of gasoline adds 6.8 pounds of weight to the rear of the car, causing some slight changes in its handling as you drive.

## Fuel Summary

**Full Tank:** Extra weight slows car slightly.

**Empty Tank:** Car develops slight "push" (understeer).

# Spoiler Adjustments

Your stock car is equipped with a front air dam skirt at the base of its nose, and a two-piece aluminum spoiler mounted on the rear deck lid. These two components can be adjusted independently to apply varying degrees of downforce to the car. Downforce is necessary to help your car "stick to the pavement" at high speeds.

As you add downforce to your car, it is important to note that you also create more drag. Think of it this way: as you circle a track in your stock car, you are driving against an air mass. As you increase the body surface that this air strikes, more drag occurs, and the car gets slower. Consequently, increasing downforce makes your car easier to drive in the turns but slows it somewhat on the straights.

## Front Air Dam Sizing

You can add more downforce to the front of your stock car by lowering the front air dam. This will help reduce understeer, making your car easier to drive in the turns. Top speed, however, will suffer somewhat due to the increase in overall drag. When the air dam is raised, more air is directed beneath the car, providing more top speed while sacrificing some grip up front.

The front air dam is affixed with screws to the skirting around the nose of the car. Instead round holes, the screws go through verticle slots punched along the length of the dam. Technicians loosen these screws and slide the air dam up or down to the desired height, then retighten the fasteners. You can perform this adjustment yourself by selecting **Spoilers** from the **Garage Menu**. Choose **Front Air Dam**, and raise or lower the setting to achieve results.

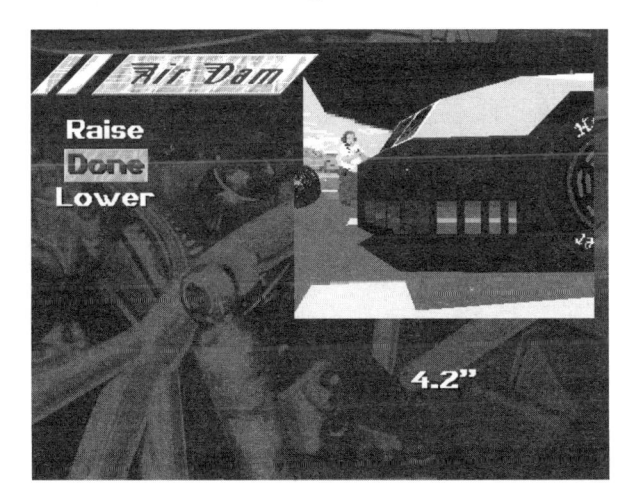

By choosing "Lower," the air dam is lowered, providing more downforce. Choose "Raise" to raise the air dam, reducing drag. Numbers in the lower right corner of screen indicate current air dam height off ground, in inches. This number will decrease as you choose "Lower," bringing the air dam closer to the ground.

*In The Garage: Tune Ups And Bench Racing*

## Rear Spoiler Angle

Increasing the spoiler angle of attack creates more downforce on the rear of the car. This added downforce keeps the car's back end from losing grip in the corners, enabling the driver to apply more throttle. However, drag created by the higher spoiler angle will extract a price on the car's top speed as well as its fuel economy.

Adjustments to the spoiler are purely manual; a crew member repeatedly bangs the aluminum wing with a mallet, bending it to achieve the desired angle. NASCAR Racing makes this job a little easier. Simply select Spoilers from the Garage or Pit Menu. Choose **Rear Spoiler**, and adjust the angle of attack up or down to provide the desired effect.

Choose "More" to raise the angle of the rear spoiler, providing more downforce to the rear of the car. Choose "Less" to lower the spoiler, reducing downforce. The numbers in the lower right corner of the screen indicate spoiler angle, in degrees. As "More" is depressed, this value will increase.

*In The Garage: Tune Ups And Bench Racing*

## Spoiler Summary

**More Air Dam:** Used to correct "pushing" condition. Lowers front air dam closer to the ground, creating more downforce up front. Increases drag.

**Less Air Dam:** Used to correct "loose" condition and/or pick up additional top speed. Raises front air dam up away from ground, reducing front downforce and drag.

**More Rear Spoiler:** Used to alleviate "loose" condition by improving grip at rear wheels. Generates more downforce on rear deck lid by raising spoiler's angle. Increases drag, reduces top speed.

**Less Rear Spoiler:** Used to improve top speed and alleviate "pushing" condition. Reduces downforce and drag on rear deck lid by lowering spoiler's angle.

**Note:** More downforce increases drag and slows the car. Tires run hotter, car may be easier to drive. Less downforce reduces drag and increases top speed. Set the car up such that it can be driven on any line of the race track, with minimal downforce.

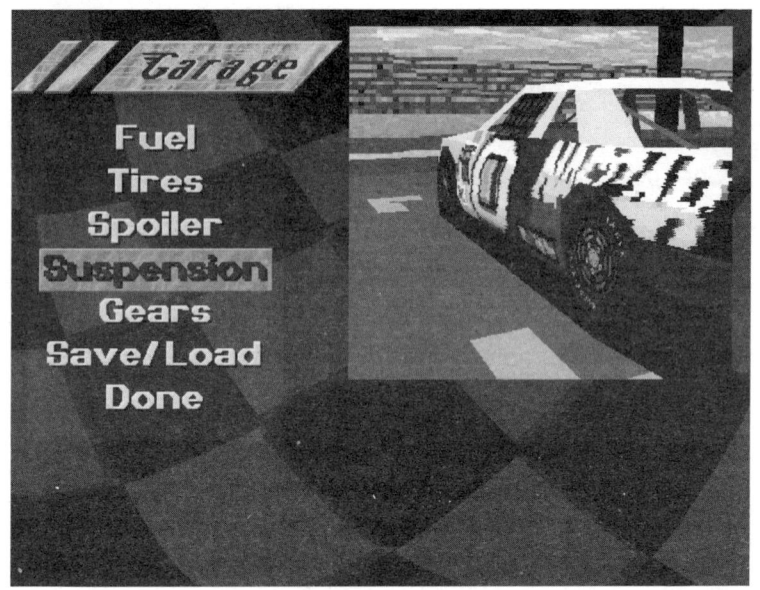

## Suspension Science

You might think NASCAR teams spend the majority of race prep time on the engine; however, the car's chassis actually hogs most of the attention. After all, the top speed obtainable by your stock car is directly related to how much grip your tires can find. What good are seven-hundred ponies under the hood if their hooves can't bite cleanly into the earth as they gallop?

When you make adjustments to the chassis of your stock car, you're trying to improve the car's overall handling characteristics. Chassis setups may vary greatly from track to track. Weather reports may also lead you to build a collection of chassis tunings for each track. The chassis you like at Bristol in April may stink up the place there in August.

# Front Wheel Camber

When you're diving into a high-speed corner, several factors affect your car's suspension. The car's weight shifts toward the outside of the turn while downforce helps press the car to the track. And if that corner happens to be steeply banked (like Bristol's are) your car may actually weigh three times greater than normal at that moment. All of these elements affect the camber of your wheels. **Camber** is a term used to describe how perpendicular your tires are to the roadway. Since cambers change under the punishing load of high speed conditions, proper settings are based on what the car does on the track, not how it sits in the garage.

In order to make sound camber adjustments, you'll need to pay close attention to tire temperatures. Begin by climbing into the car for a few laps at full race speed (three to five laps on short tracks & road courses, five to eight laps on super speedways). This will warm the tires up, giving you accurate temperature readings.

After your warmup laps, head back to your garage by pressing [ESC] while in the cockpit. Select **Suspension/Camber** from the **Garage Menu**. Take a look at the right front wheel first. The temperatures displayed onscreen will reflect your warmup effort. The tire thermometer will actually show you three temperatures, taken from the inner, middle and outer sections of the tire surface. Under ideal conditions, these temperatures should read identical. If one side of the tire is considerably hotter than the other, camber adjustment is necessary. If the outer edge of the tire is hotter, bring the top of the tire in a little by decreasing the current camber value.

If the inner edge of the tire is hotter, it is adjusted too far toward the negative camber side. Apply more positive camber to correct the situation. Remember, your goal is to strive for even temperatures on each side of the tire. After examining the right front wheel, check and adjust the left front camber in the same manner.

**Note:** Tire temperatures do not change while in the garage making camber adjustments. Following adjustment, you'll need to return to the track for a few laps in order to acquire new temperature readings. It may take a few trips back to the garage to get camber settings "dialed in."

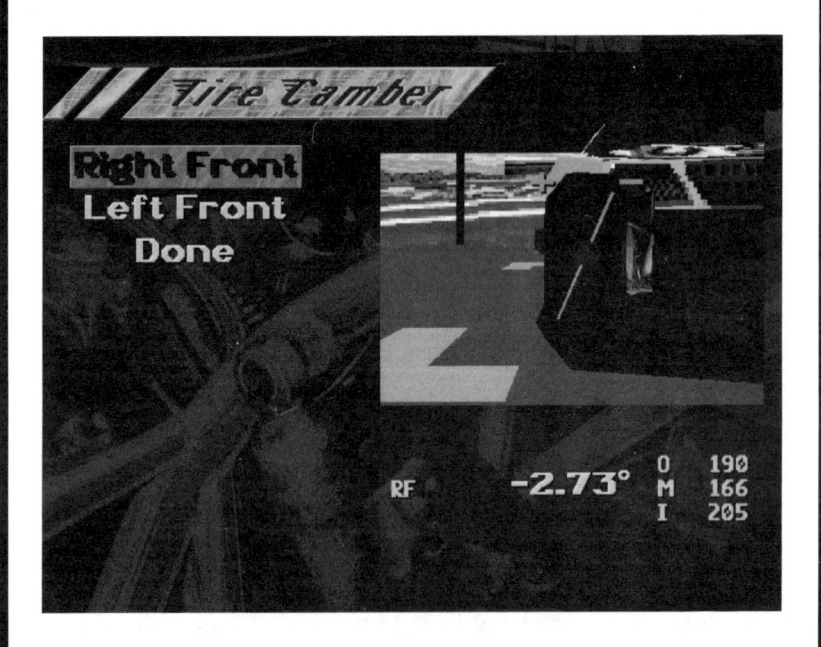

Positive **Camber** adjustments tip the top of the tire away from the car, while negative adjustments bring the wheel's top closer to the car. Since stock cars use a straight axle on the rear, you cannot adjust camber of the rear wheels. Generally, the only way to do this would be to bend the axle itself.

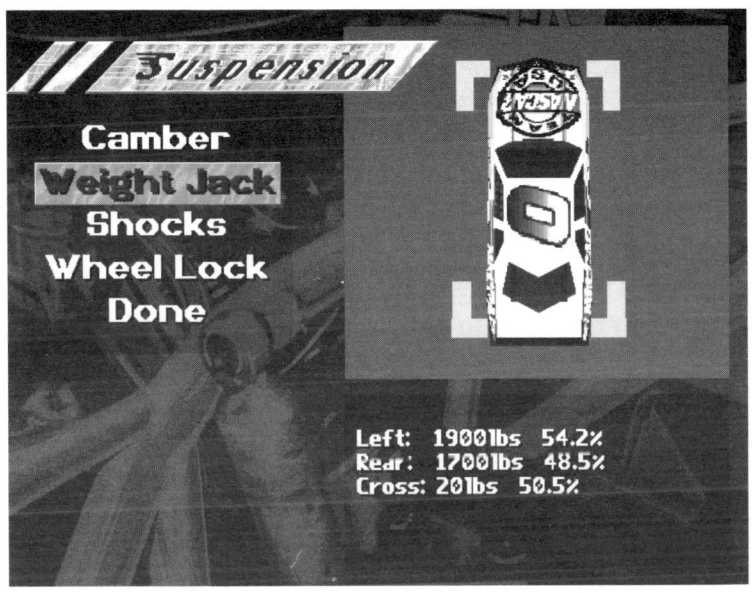

# Weights & Wedges

The weight of your car shifts constantly in various directions as you drive your stock car. For instance, when you accelerate, more of the car's weight shifts toward the rear. When you brake, the weight tends to shift forward, pressing the hood of your stock car down. When you turn left, weight shifts to the right. When you turn right, the load goes to the left. The greater your *action*, the greater the car's *reaction*.

Confused? Don't worry, it gets easier. Let's start with a completely balanced car. The total weight is 3500 lbs., so that means the weight at each wheel would equal 875 lbs. The front half of the car would weigh 1750 lbs., and so would the rear. The left side would weigh in at 1750, and so would

*In The Garage: Tune Ups And Bench Racing*

the right. Incidentally, NASCAR uses a special scale that measures weight under each wheel of your car simultaneously, accurate to within an ounce!

Now, we'll make a few adjustments to redistribute the car's weight, where it's needed most. Choose **Weight Jack** from the **Suspension Menu**. You'll be presented with three options: **Left Bias, Rear Bias and Cross Weight**. We'll cover each one to help get you started.

## Left Bias Adjustment

Let's assume that you want to adjust the left-side weight of the car for a track like Darlington. Because the car will be spending a great deal of time turning left around Darlington's treacherous banks, your car's weight will be thrown to the right a good bit. By starting with more weight on the left side of the car (NASCAR limits you to 1900 lbs. on any one half of the car, of course) you can offset this weight shift and carry more speed through the turn. By raising the value of the **Left Bias** on the **Weight Jack Menu**, you are increasing the static weight on the left side of the car.

In general, your stock car is well under the 3500 lb. minimum weight. NASCAR teams bring the weight up to specs by adding slabs of lead to the car's frame. By positioning these slabs to the left-side of the car, the weight becomes dominant on the left. This is also known as a *"Ballast"* adjustment. Car weight is one of the most common corners that race teams try to shave. According to Gary Nelson, NASCAR's Chief Inspector, *"Everybody wants the car as light as they can get it. Some people have tried to bring their cars on the scales at 3450 lbs. They'd stick a box of tools behind the* driver's seat to get the weight up to 3500 lbs., but we look for that stuff right away. The penalties for breaking the rules are pretty high, so most teams don't outright cheat, they just work on the gray areas." NASCAR Racing prevents you from breaking any weight rules. Heck, if we didn't, Nelson's boys'd be all over you!

Choose "More" to slide the ballast to the left side of the race car. The current percentage of left side weight is shown as well. 1900 lbs. is the maximum weight allowable on any half of the car. Left ballast can be reduced all the way down to 1600 lbs., but this can cause the car to behave erratically.

*In The Garage: Tune Ups And Bench Racing*

## Rear Bias Adjustment

At big tracks like Talladega, your car is in a constant state of high speed, so more weight will be shifted to the rear of the car. This would make your car "loose," or oversteer (rear wheels lose grip first in turns). However, if you have more weight in the front of the car to begin with, the load that shifts toward the rear will be minimized, thus balancing the car under high speed conditions. NASCAR driver Dave Marcis explains, *"The front percentage of the race car at, say, Talladega would perhaps be around fifty-two-and-a-half to fifty-three percent. If you were at a race track like Martinsville, the front percentage of the car would only be about fifty-point-five to fifty-one percent."* Martinsville Speedway is just over a half-mile in length. The speeds are slower, meaning the shift of weight from front to rear that occurs is much less than it would be at Talladega.

**Rear Bias**, or Ballast, is adjusted by the race team inside the garage. Mechanics move frame-mounted lead slabs forward or backward accordingly, to create the desired weight displacement.

You will probably want the rear weight to be below 1750 lbs., starting with more weight in the front of the race car. Choose **"Less"** to achieve this.

*In The Garage: Tune Ups And Bench Racing*

## Adjusting Cross Weight

You can adjust the front-to-rear and left-to-right weight ratios on your stock car, and that's all well and good. But what if you want to change the car's weight at a specific wheel, for instance the left rear? That's where **"Cross Weight"** comes into play.

Because the majority of corners you drive will turn left, it would be ideal to get more of the car's weight on the left rear wheel. This would help the rear wheels grip better in a high-speed left turn (the weight shifting to the right would balance the rear axle). At the same time, weight would increase on the right front wheel, an already heavily-stressed tire.

**Cross Weight** adjustment, also called *"wedge,"* is made by "tipping" one corner of the car up or down. For instance, if you lower the left-rear corner of the car, that wheel will weigh more, because more of the car's weight is pointed toward it. By shortening or lengthening certain springs on your car, you can tip that cross weight in the direction you want. Your team can do this operation in the garage or pit area- it requires nothing more than turning a big screw.

It works like this: Each spring on your car has a cover on top, and each spring cover has a threaded rod going through it. These rods, called "screw jacks," extend upward for easy access. The rear screw jacks can be reached through the rear window glass. The front screw jacks are located under the hood, just inside each wheel. One complete rotation of a screw jack is called a "round" in NASCAR terminology. If you hear a team say they "took a couple of rounds out of the left-rear wheel," that means they loosened the left rear screw jack two full rotations.

Shot of a screw jack, connected to the top of the spring. As the threaded rod is turned, the spring gets shorter, because the spring cover pushes it downward. This changes the ride-height of the car at that wheel. (Vandergriff Photo)

Each "round" equals approximately five pounds of weight. Start with the cross weight at zero (no wedge added). If your car is "loose" (rear-end loses grip too early), increase the cross weight. This will "tighten" your car and make it tend to "push" (understeer). After each adjustment, run a few laps then check the right front tire temperature to make sure it isn't going to be overstressed. Keep in mind that as you add wedge, the left rear and right front corners of the car will increase in weight. The right rear and left front corners will get lighter. Check these tires to make sure they aren't running too cold.

122  **In The Garage: Tune Ups And Bench Racing**

# The Weighting Game

NASCAR rules state that each side of the car must weight at least 1600 lbs. That means 1900 lbs. is the largest amount of bias you can generate. Left and rear ballast settings should be considered coarse adjustments, while cross weight (wedge) should be considered a fine adjustment. Get the biases where you want them during test sessions. Use the cross weight adjustment to fine tune the car to fit current track conditions.

## Weight Jacking Summary

**Left Bias Benefits:** Increasing this value puts more weight on the left side of the car, helping balance the chassis as you turn left. Correct setting improves tire grip in turns.

**Left Bias Side Effects:** When your car is driven around steep banks, gravity makes it weigh more, particularly the left side. An overload could rob you of some speed in the corners. Left side tires may overheat and wear quicker, while right-side tires run too cold.

**Rear Bias Benefits:** Decreasing this value puts more weight up front, where you want it. Balances the car under acceleration.

**Rear Bias Side Effects:** Too much rear weight makes the car "loose," too little makes it "push."

**Cross Weight:** Increase this setting to "tighten" the car up if it's too "loose." Decrease this setting to correct understeer.

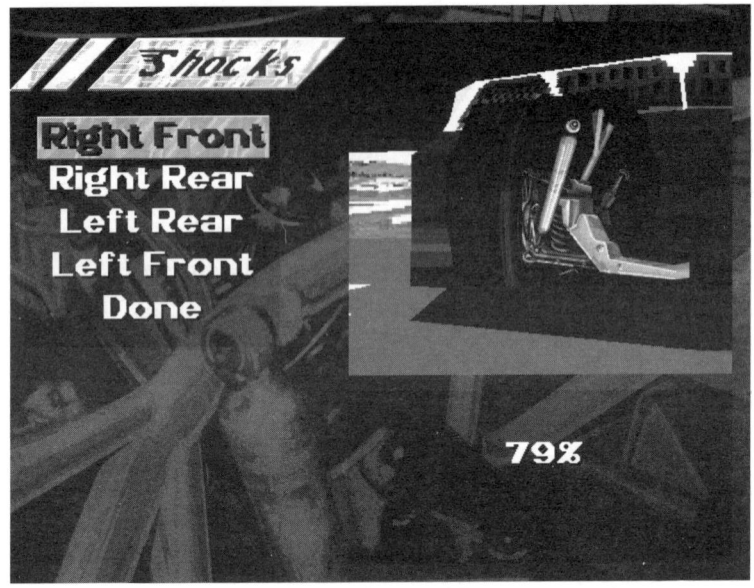

## Shock Stiffness

Gas-filled shock absorbers are installed at each wheel of your stock car. Aside from minimizing the little bumps and jounces experienced on the race track, shocks play a key role in stabilizing the car's chassis during turns.

When you turn left, centrifugal force causes your car's chassis to shift weight to the right. Conversely, right turns cause the chassis weight to be shifted left. When you accelerate, the car's weight shifts toward the rear; braking causes the weight to shift forward. Every time the car's weight shifts in one of these directions, you're losing grip somewhere.

By adjusting the stiffness of each shock absorber, you can improve the cornering performance of the race car. Stiffer shocks cause the chassis to "reset" quicker after a transference of weight. However, this added responsiveness can lead a driver to overreact. Softer shock settings mean that chassis roll will last longer as the weight transfer dampens out gradually. While stiffer suspension may improve the car's response, a softer chassis tends to be more forgiving.

Individually speaking, if you adjust a shock to a stiffer value as compared to the others, more weight will transfer at that wheel and diminish its tire grip. Adjusting a shock to a softer setting minimizes load transfer at that wheel, providing better traction. As a rule of thumb, you'll want the rear shocks to be softer than the front ones in order to keep the car from getting "loose."

## The Adjustment Process

The first time a car is set up from scratch, the typical race team will make the front end very stiff, while using very soft settings on the rear. This results in understeer, or in other words, a "push." From there the team can tweak the suspension stiffness to offer the most consistent feel for a specific track. Top speeds, tire temperatures and track banking must all be taken into account to properly manage weight transfers. If your car pushes too much, stiffen the rear end some. If the car feels too loose, soften the rear and/or stiffen the front.

Choose **Shocks** from the **Suspension** section of the **Garage Menu**. Select which shock you are going to adjust. The number located in the lower right part of the screen represents the current shock stiffness. The higher you move the percentage, the stiffer the shock becomes. Adjust each shock absorber individually, then choose **"Done."**

## Shock Theory

Many NASCAR teams feel that by using softer spring/shock combinations at the rear end, they can cause the tail of the car to ride lower. This would drop the spoiler down in the wind, reducing drag and increasing the car's speed. This theory is questioned by some, because the speed gained from the spoiler reduction may be lost in the additional understeer you'd pick up. Hey, you're the head wrench- if it makes you quicker then go with it.

## Shock Summary

**Softer Shock:** Reduces weight transfer at that wheel. Car becomes less responsive as chassis takes longer to reset after a turn. More "forgiving" to drive, softer rear shocks may lower spoiler angle when driving.

**Stiffer Shock:** Increases weight transfer at that wheel. Handling becomes more responsive, car can feel a little "slippery" as chassis snaps back into place after a turn.

With the hood raised, you can easily see that the front shocks are firmly bolted at the top to the frame of the car. Each wheel of the car has a single gas-filled shock mounted to it. (Papyrus Photo)

# Wheel Lock

By using different gear combinations in the steering box, your crew can alter the turning radius of your stock car. Choose **Wheel Lock** from the Suspension section of the Garage menu. Highlight **More** if you want a sharper turning pattern; **Less** allows you to shorten the steering radius.

If there were only one racing line (best path around a track) and you knew you'd never have to stray from it, you could probably run the same steering gear throughout a season. But short tracks and road courses create heavy traffic and drivers often have to drive a variety of racing lines to stay up front. These tracks demand sharper turning capabilities, thus more steering angle. Drivers don't spend as much time turning at the megatracks like Talladega, so less steering angle is desired to help keep control.

*In The Garage: Tune Ups And Bench Racing*

## What It Doesn't Do

Don't try to compensate for a bad setup by making last-minute adjustments to the steering gear! If your car is pushing, try stiffening the rear shocks or lowering the front air dam. The **Wheel Lock** adjustment should only be made in the interest of driver experience and track type; it will do little to correct other problems stemming from improper setups.

## Wheel Lock Summary

**More Wheel Lock:** Increases turning radius of the car. Too much wheel lock can cause driver to over-react and burn tires up quicker.

**Less Wheel Lock:** Decreases turning radius of your stock car. Driving with less wheel lock than necessary is a dangerous condition, and should be corrected. Failure to do so will have you painting the track's walls with your stock car.

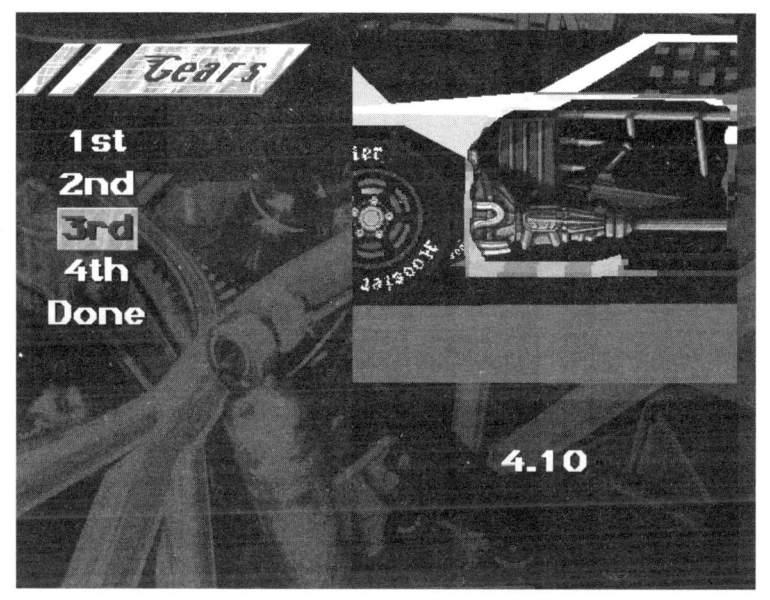

## Gear Ratios

Every serious driver wants more top speed in their cars at super speedways like Talladega, while the two-footed short tracks such as Martinsville demand a package that emphasizes acceleration. In order to meet these needs, NASCAR teams change the gear combinations used in the rear differential or transmission.

NASCAR teams keep a sizeable stash of cogs around. So many gears, so little time... (Vandergriff Photo)

Taller gears are used to generate more top speed. When you're on a big track you'll want to keep your foot on the floor and stay in fourth-gear all day. Your stock car's driveshaft will need to turn about three times to produce one revolution of the rear

*In The Garage: Tune Ups And Bench Racing* 129

wheels. Under these conditions, taller ratios will meet your need for speed.

Shorter gears tighten the power curve generated by your engine. Shorter ratios will cause the driveshaft to turn four or five times to produce a single revolution of the drive wheels. This kind of gear setup is useful on the short tracks, where top speed is not the issue. Passing other cars on a short track often takes several patient laps, executed through a series of short stabs back and forth on the brake and gas pedals. Your car'd better have quick bursts of power if you want to succeed at this kind of "bullring racing."

Select **Gears** from the **Garage Menu**. Highlight the gear you would like to adjust. Choose **Shorter** if you want a smaller gear that produces more rpms, and quicker acceleration. Choose **Taller** if you want to get more top speed, while conceding some acceleration. If your oil pressure warning light flickers constantly while you're in fourth gear, select **Taller** to provide fewer engine rpms.

## Gear Ratios Summary

**Shorter Gear:** More rpms/acceleration. Tighter gearing gets you up to speed quicker.

**Taller Gear:** Slower acceleration, possibly more top speed. If your engine continuously runs too hot, try lengthening the gear ratios.

## Options
### (From The Garage Menu)

Each track that came with your copy of NASCAR Racing has three predefined car setups, built specifically for that track, ready for use. These setups are called **Easy, Fast** and **Ace**. You may load any of these car settings from within the garage; you may then drive them as is, or tweak them a little to fit your driving style.

The **Easy** setup provides beginners with a slower car that is simple to drive. This car would qualify near the back of the starting grid. The **Fast** setup is an intermediate package that will be competitive on some tracks. The **Ace** setup is the fastest pretuned car. Drivers using the **Ace** file should be ready to tangle with the hotshoes up front. This setting file could put you on the pole under optimum conditions.

This is how a stock car begins its life- the metal chassis and roll cage is completely designed and welded together from scratch. The chassis is suspended by a jig, which allows the welder to rotate the chassis for easy access. (Vandergriff Photo)

You may also save any number of your favorite car settings to disk; you can then reload them anytime for driving or further tuning. You may give these files any name you wish, but be advised- if you choose the name **Easy, Fast** or **Ace** you will overwrite these files. We recommend names that say something about that particular setup. For example, **QUAL208** to indicate a qualifying setup that runs 208 mph.

You can use the **Delete** command to get rid of old or unwanted setups. Highlight **Delete**, then choose the setup you wish to erase.

All setting files are stored in the subdirectory of the track they belong to. For instance, a setting you create at Talladega, called **TALL210** will not appear on the **Garage/Options/Load Menu** at Atlanta. If you are familiar with DOS, you may want to copy or rename setting files for use on other tracks. You could also swap them with friends. Setting files are denoted by the **.STG** extension. For further information, consult your DOS owner's manual.

Marshall Teague sits behind the wheel of his Hudson Hornet on Daytona Beach in 1951. The front quarter of the car is taped over to repel sand. Teague's brother painted the graphics on the car shortly before this shot was taken. Hudson merged with auto giant AMC in the late fifties, and the line was discontinued by 1958. (Daytona Racing Archives)

# Kings Of The Beach

Daytona Beach, February, 1953. Eisenhower is President, "From Here To Eternity" is playing at the box office and a gallon of gasoline costs less than 35¢. The glaring Florida sun illuminates the sandy shoreline, and the Atlantic wind bellows from seemingly every direction as the ocean tide rolls seaward.

This is the first time you've seen Florida, but you're not here to collect unusual shells, you're here to run over them. You, your brother-in-law and two of his buddies you've never met have traveled south together to take a shot at owning a piece of auto racing glory.

The car you hope to take the checkered flag in happens to be one of the more popular models in stock car racing, a Hudson Hornet. Although a bit large (over four tons), the Hornet has a low center of gravity.

*American History: The Evolution Of NASCAR Racing*

You've taped over the headlights, fastened the doors shut with some rope and removed the hub caps. Devoid of sponsorships, the only graphics on the car are the wash-off numbers you personally brushed on the night before. For the race you'll leave the license plates on the car, too. Heck, you've still got to drive 'er home after the race!

You'll be going up against names like Teague, Thomas and Flock and, oh yes, that Petty kid- not Richard, but his father Lee. You only hope you don't bend the car up, since you promised the wife she could have it for a shopping trip upon your return.

As you can see, the early days of NASCAR were simple and often ungratifying. These were the genuine "Run what ya brung" days of racing. Many of that era's drivers were also the sponsor, team owner, car builder and head mechanic. There wasn't a whole lot of money in the sport back then. Few drivers had contracts, and most worked day jobs in garages, gas stations and dealerships. NASCAR as an organization was only five years old, under-funded and limited to a region below the Mason-Dixon line. But why Daytona, and why the South? Why not some of the existing racing hotbeds like Milwaukee or Indianapolis?

# The Birthplace Of Speed

Ormond Beach is located just north of Daytona, on the Atlantic coast of Florida. Before the Bonneville Salt Flats became popularized as a mecca for speed, Ormond Beach held that distinction. Its miles of wide, hard-packed sand that stretched forth along the shoreline provided a perfect setting for land speed record competition.

Early speed stars: Sir Malcolm Campbell (l) with Barney Oldfield at Ormond Beach. (Daytona Racing Archives)

In 1902 the first automobile speed record runs were staged on Ormond Beach. Each year after that, car makers and race drivers would descend on Ormond for a shot at the speed title. Eventually the course was expanded to include a section of Daytona Beach. Famous faces like Barney Oldfield, Frank Lockhart and Ralph DePalma made the annual trek south for "speed weeks," each one eager to better the other.

Sir Malcolm Campbell brought his famous "Bluebird" race car to Ormond in the early thirties, and made several attempts to set world speed records. In 1935, Campbell topped three-hundred miles an hour, but it wasn't at Ormond Beach- it was several thousand miles west

Sir Malcolm Campbell's famous "Bluebird" in a speed run on Ormond Beach, 1935. (Daytona Racing Archives)

**American History: The Evolution Of NASCAR Racing 135**

**OFFICIALLY LICENSED BY**
///////*NASCAR*.

at Bonneville. Attention quickly shifted to the Salt Flats as a better speed venue, and interest in Ormond Beach as a speed site evaporated.

The city fathers of Ormond decided to create a winter stock car race to replace the speed trials. The man they charged with the job of organizing it was Sig Haugdahl, a former speed pioneer who was the first man to travel 180 mph on Ormond in 1922. Haugdahl is also believed to be the first driver to balance his tires by using weights mounted on the rims.

Haugdahl created a stock car course by measuring a mile in the sand, using a mile of highway A1A that runs parallel to the coast, and joining the two with a pair of short chutes cut through the sand dunes. The finished product was 3.2 miles in length; the first race would be a 250-miler. The AAA contest board sanctioned the event and scheduled it for March 8, 1936.

The original Daytona Beach race course, as seen from the air. The track was later lengthened from 3.2 miles to 4.1. After the first race, the chutes were graded with marl, a clay-like compound. (Daytona Racing Archives)

**136** *American History: The Evolution Of NASCAR Racing*

The $5,000 purse drew some of the top names in the sport, including Indy 500 champion Bill Cummings. Though a financial success, the race had to be shortened when the chutes got so chewed up that the tow trucks couldn't pull everyone out of trouble fast enough. Milt Marion, driving a Ford, was declared the winner. He averaged just under 49 mph. Marion's car was prepared by the race's fifth-place finisher, a lanky twenty-seven-year-old Virginian named Bill France.

## France's Vision

William H. G. (Bill) France, Sr. first arrived in Daytona in 1934. He had decided a racing mechanic's life would be more lucrative in the South, so he loaded the family's belongings in a trailer and, along with wife Anne and young sons Bill, Jr. and Jim, set out for Miami. The family stopped in the Ormond Beach area and eventually settled in Daytona, where Bill got a job as a mechanic.

By 1936, France was eager to be involved in the organization of the stock car event, and he even helped Haugdahl lay out the course. After finishing a respectable fifth in the race, Bill France took what he learned on the beach that day and began to build upon it. He

The late Bill France, Sr., founding father of NASCAR and the Daytona International Speedway. Under France's guidance, the sport achieved much needed consistency and credibility. (Daytona Racing Archives)

American History: The Evolution Of NASCAR Racing 137

eventually became one of the race's promoters, steering the event to greater financial success until WWII suspended the competition.

By the mid-forties, the war was over and Bill France began organizing a small series of races in the south. He now knew several promoters, drivers, mechanics and sports writers. He gathered a group of these associates together on December 14, 1947, in a smoke-filled room at the Streamline Motel in Daytona Beach. NASCAR (National Association for Stock Car Auto Racing) was officially born out of this meeting. The late Red Vogt, an experienced mechanic is credited with devising the name.

NASCAR is born out of this meeting at the Streamline Motel in Daytona Beach, 1949. Bill France (in white shirt) is seated at the head of the table next to Bill Tuthill. France told the group he felt the sport needed a national points system, insurance coverage for drivers, and a low-cost format of events. He also advised the panel that Sunday shows would draw the biggest crowds, allowing race-minded drivers the time to earn a living during the work week. The group responded favorably, and by the next day had named a board of directors (with France as President) and appointed committees to administrate technical and competition issues. Just two months later, Red Byron won the first NASCAR sanctioned event, the 1948 Daytona Beach Race. (Daytona Racing Archives)

The NASCAR charter immediately created a points championship for drivers, sanctioned a series of races (including the Daytona Beach race) and began competition in 1948. Many of the first NASCAR drivers quickly developed the skills necessary to be competitive in stock car racing.

## Day Of The Dirt Devils

Aside from that paved one-mile stretch of A1A at Daytona, most of the early NASCAR events were contested on dirt. NASCAR got its first asphalt superspeedway in 1950. Darlington Raceway opened its doors to the young division, hosting the inaugural Southern 500. What is now Daytona International Speedway was still nothing more than a large parcel of swampy land. Still, the Daytona Beach Race remained NASCAR's flagship.

The pock-marked beach surface caused the cars to pitch and roll wildly as they engaged the chutes. Weight jacking wasn't around yet, as you can see by the Nash's (41) chassis torsion. (Daytona Racing Archives)

American History: The Evolution Of NASCAR Racing  139

**OFFICIALLY LICENSED BY NASCAR**

Stock cars of the fifties resembled clumsy behemoths, staying forever loose on the unkempt dirt surfaces they raced on. Slipping, sliding and banging fenders became a common spectacle at every NASCAR event, since tires and suspension components had not been developed for such conditions. In fact, the bumpy dirt surfaces broke shock absorbers so frequently that racers mounted two shocks on each wheel.

NASCAR began experimenting with several new divisions to increase the sport's impact. A speedway category for open-wheel cars came into the fold in 1952. The cars had open canopies, but used stock-block engines. The concept was considered to be a sharp departure from NASCAR's original path, and the division proved to be short-lived.

Two years later, several west-coast tracks were added in an effort to bring NASCAR racing to fans on a nation-wide level.

Obie Chupp gets it going the wrong way as Herb Thomas tries to sneak by. Those roof flaps oughta be kicking in any minute... (Daytona Racing Archives)

**Marshall Teague: Hudson's Factory Champ**

Marshall Teague was a rare breed. He could pilot a car as well as any driver going. At the same time, he was a successful head mechanic, often labeled as the first innovater of the NASCAR chassis. He brought the fabled Hudson Hornet to the sport, scoring back-to-back wins in the Daytona Beach Race in '51 and '52. He is also believed to be the pioneer of legitimate sponsorship involvement in NASCAR competition. (Daytona Racing Archives)

140 *American History: The Evolution Of NASCAR Racing*

Thanks to the appeal of stock car racing, NASCAR was beginning to polish its image. What had once been a notch above rustling on the scale of respectability was quietly becoming a financial success. After all, the stock car was everybody's car, the family sedan with an attitude. People could relate easily to the stock car, because they owned similar vehicles themselves.

Drivers made some interesting choices for race cars in the early days. The car in the foreground is a...don't laugh...Studebaker. (Daytona Racing Archives)

## Detroit Comes Calling

When Marshall Teague introduced the Hudson Hornet to NASCAR in 1951, he became the first driver to have the backing of an automaker. Teague spent much time in the Hudson workshop, developing dual carburetion and refining the car's six-cylinder flathead engine. Teague also owned a filling station, and persuaded the parent oil company to back his racing efforts.

When driver Herb Thomas teamed with Teague in the early fifties, the combination proved explosive for Hudson. The Hornet, or "Teaguemobiles" as they were known in racing circles, began stinging the NASCAR competition, recording twenty-seven wins in thirty-four races. Marshall Teague himself won the Daytona Beach event back-to-back, in 1951 and 1952.

**American History: The Evolution Of NASCAR Racing**

Other manufacturers joined the fray in the mid-fifties: Ford, Mercury, Pontiac, Chevy, Chrysler and Oldsmobile. Auto parts makers were getting in as well. Spark plug, tire, shock, and oil companies all began supplying race teams with merchandise, technology and a few bucks.

As the factory involvement brought higher speeds, NASCAR moved to enhance the safety of its drivers. Rules were gradually improved to accommodate the tracks and equipment that existed. For example roll cages, which had been nothing more than crude two-by-fours or hollow aluminum, were mandated to be heavy steel tubing. Slick tires, however, were still disallowed in the sport.

**NASCAR's Ragtop Division**

In the late fifties, NASCAR actually had a convertible division. The class allowed spectators a better glimpse of their favorite drivers in action.

In the photo above, Curtis Turner's Ford (26) leads Tim Flock's Mercury (15) through the famous north turn on the Daytona Beach Course. The convertibles arrived when NASCAR merged with SAFE, a racing organization out of the midwest. (Daytona Racing Archives)

Most of the teams still had only two or three employees, including the driver. Pit workers or garage mechanics were usually unpaid volunteers, working for nothing more than the satisfaction of a job well done or the occassional free beers awarded when things went well. And many of the drivers towed or drove their race cars to the track themselves.

# The Superspeedway Era

When Paul Goldsmith took the checkered flag at the sands of Daytona in 1958, it marked the final chapter in beach racing. Bill France had mustered enough civic and financial support to finally build his dream come true: a permanent superspeedway in Daytona. As early as 1949, France had expressed fears that the beach property would eventually wind up in the hands of hotel and resort developers, and he was also miffed by the bull moose crowd in Indianapolis. NASCAR had Darlington, but it needed something more.

France wanted a track unlike any other: a two-and-a-half mile tri-oval with sweeping 31 degree banked ends, "as steep as they could lay asphalt," he would later say. The Daytona International Speedway opened in time for speedweek in February, 1959. Many of the drivers were perplexed at the sudden jolt of speed the big track produced. For instance, Fireball Roberts blazed around the track at an unheard of 149.70 mph pace. Roberts was testing a modified 1957 Ford that used a 325 c.id. engine to generate 430 horsepower. Cotton Owens qualified for the Daytona 500 at 143 mph, over 30 mph faster than the speeds churned out on the old beach course!

Photo Finish: Bill France studied this photo and some film clips he'd gathered from the media in order to determine the first Daytona 500 winner. He eventually ruled that Lee Petty's Olds (42) had nipped Johnny Beauchamp's Ford (73) at the line, by a bumper. The exciting finish proved to be a feather in France's cap; can you imagine how much longer it might have taken for the superspeedways to catch on, had Petty won by nine laps? (Daytona Racing Archives)

**OFFICIALLY LICENSED BY**
///////NASCAR.

It seemed Bill France had though of everything...except a photo finish. The first Daytona 500 ended in a dead heat, with Lee Petty being declared the winner three days later, only after France had time to collect and study films and photos of the finish.

One year later, new superspeedways opened in Atlanta, Georgia, and Charlotte, North Carolina. Coinciding with NASCAR's move to these asphalt ovals, the Detroit auto makers had begun putting a premium on sleeker, V-8 driven cars, abandoning the "sherman tank" rounded look of the forties and fifties. Gone was the "Fabulous" Hudson Hornet. Gone were the bulky rear fenders that left only the bottom-third of the rear wheels exposed. Gone was the beach. And gone were the constant challenges that had arisen when trying to patch together race schedules without a clear cut stable of tracks accessible to the NASCAR organization.

Banjo Matthews (L) readies an engine for his driver, A. J. Foyt (R). (Daytona Racing Archives)

### Master Mechanics

As star drivers with true skill began to emerge, so did the ingenious men who built the cars they won races in. The Holman-Moody Ford Team, Bud Moore, Cotton Owens, Ray Fox and Banjo Matthews each earned the quiet respect of the NASCAR drivers they helped make look good on Sunday afternoons.

Some of these men remain active in stock car racing to this day: Banjo still builds NASCAR race cars out of his shop in Asheville, N.C., while Bud Moore owns a NASCAR Winston Cup race team.

This photo shows what garages looked like when the cars were still bought off the lot. (Daytona Racing Archives)

**OFFICIALLY LICENSED BY NASCAR**

Instead, NASCAR ushered in its speedway era with a fresh stable of new cars and young talent. The list reads like a hall of fame roster: Fireball Roberts, Richard Petty, Fred Lorenzen, Curtis Turner, Ned Jarrett, Joe Weatherly, Junior Johnson (before he was a car owner he won 50 NASCAR races), Marvin Panch, Speedy Thompson and David Pearson.

ABC dispatched their mobile television trucks to Daytona on Independence Day in 1961, airing the Firecracker 250 race on its "Wide World Of Sports" program. It marked the first nationwide telecast of a NASCAR event. David Pearson took the checkered flag, and America finally got a look at the cars and stars that were captivating the South.

Bumper-to-bumper, door-to-door driving on the speedways became a NASCAR fixture, and so did something else— driver superstitions. Little Joe Weatherly (a former AMA motorcycle champ) feared no one on the race track, but he

### Glenn Roberts: NASCAR's "Fireball"

One of NASCAR's first true superstars, Fireball Roberts became a legend. Hailing from Daytona, Roberts racked up 32 NASCAR victories in his career. He earned the nickname "Fireball" as a fastball pitcher for Seabreeze High School, and was introduced to stock car racing through his friend, fellow Daytonan Marshall Teague.

In 1962, sportswriters awarded Roberts the prestigious Hickok award, edging out Arnold Palmer and Wilt Chamberlain for the prize. He had won the Daytona 500 that year, becoming the first driver to win the pole for the event three consecutive years. He also traveled to Le Mans that year to compete in the 24 hours race, finishing a respectable sixth.

Though considered ace of the speedways, he had never won at Charlotte, and tragically he lost his life following an accident there during the 1964 World 600. (Daytona Racing Archives Photos).

*American History: The Evolution Of NASCAR Racing* 145

had an intense dislike for the color green, as well as the number thirteen. Weatherly once had a track superintendent change the color of a green sign located near the start/finish line before he would get in the race car. On another occasion, Weatherly qualified his car thirteenth, but refused to compete in the race until they renumbered his slot "12A."

Although tales like these are great stock car folklore, NASCAR needed this kind of unexpected flavor to establish a colorful presence with its following.

Tim Flock was another talented driver with a quick wit and plenty of charisma. Flock had also amassed quite a resume: one-third of the "Fabulous Flock Brothers" (Fonty, 19 wins and Bob, 4 wins being the others), Tim Flock won forty races in his NASCAR career. On July 30, 1955, he took the checkered flag at a one-hundred miler in Syracuse, N.Y. He then had himself and his racecars flown across the country to San Mateo, California, where he won a two-hundred-and-fifty miler the next day!

In 1963, Ford and Chrysler announced full-scale participation in auto racing. That year, Fred Lorenzen won $113,750 in his Ford, becoming the first NASCAR driver to earn more than $100,000 in a single year. Lorenzen placed third in the final driver's championship, behind Joe Weatherly and Richard Petty.

By the summer of '64, President Kennedy was dead, the U.S. was mired in the Vietnam conflict and the Beatles were gaining popularity with American audiences. But while the boys from Britain were busy tearing up the pop music charts, NASCAR racing was quietly blossoming into a full-fledged speedway sport, providing its fans with a stadium-like atmosphere at each event.

**OFFICIALLY LICENSED BY**
**/////// NASCAR.**

# New Stars For New Cars

In the late sixties, auto makers began building what have affectionately come to be known as "muscle cars." Huge, American V-8 engines resting on smaller, more compact chassis designs quickly became popular with NASCAR teams and the driving public. To win a pole at Daytona in 1960 you needed to average about 152 mph. By 1968, speeds were approaching 190 mph.

Coinciding with the latest offerings from Detroit, the faces that made stock car racing began to change. Some of the early greats were gradually being replaced by relative unknowns Cale Yarborough, Lee Roy Yarbrough (no relation), brothers Bobby and Donnie Allison, Buddy Baker, and Bobby Isaac. These weren't exactly household names- yet.

As his rookie driver lands the Ford safely in the pit stall, Banjo Matthews (handling lug duty at the right front wheel) and his crack crew scurry to service the car. This action is from the first race at the North Carolina Motor Speedway in 1965. The aforementioned rookie at the helm of the race car is Cale Yarborough, who later went on score seven victories at Rockingham. Note that including Banjo, there are only six men over the pit wall. (Daytona Racing Archives)

American History: The Evolution Of NASCAR Racing 147

**OFFICIALLY LICENSED BY NASCAR**

High Speed Chase: This action from the '66 Firecracker 400 race at Daytona International Speedway offers a sense of the speeds the cars were able to reach on the banking, even back then. In the top photo, the field roars by the camera coming off of turn four. In the lower photo, you can see some of the cars tucking in behind each other in order to draft. Drivers were no longer awed by the swirling currents emitted by other cars. Rookie Sam McQuagg, driving a car sponsored by a married couple from Georgia, won the race. It would be the only Grand National win of his career. (Daytona Racing Archives)

# A Year To Remember

In 1967, one NASCAR driver competed in forty-eight races, capturing an amazing forty top ten finishes. Even more startling, this same driver won twenty-seven of those races, including a string of ten in a row! NASCAR legend Richard Petty, commandeering Petty Enterprises Plymouth Satellites, tore up tracks all over the country enroute to recording the greatest single season a stock car driver has ever had.

After a year like that, it's hard to imagine there being "one that got away." However, Petty didn't get the checkered flag at the Daytona 500, Mario Andretti did. It was Andretti's only NASCAR win.

Still, Richard Petty's twenty-seven wins that season is a mark that will probably stand forever. And in a day when cars and parts were less than reliable, Petty clicked off the ten consecutive victories enroute to his second driver's championship crown, and the king was on his throne to stay. Whatever championship battles are waged in NASCAR's future, that 1967 campaign of Richard Petty's will stand as the centerpiece of stock car excellence.

The following year, David Pearson won sixteen out of forty-eight races. His duels with Richard Petty were classic, as both drivers displayed flawless reflexes behind the wheel, along with that "something extra," a special ingredient found in rare drivers that somehow pushes them to the front of nearly every race. Ironically for Pearson, Cale Yarborough drove the Wood Brothers Mercury to a new single season money winning standard, more than $136,000. Pearson would later team with the Wood Brothers to produce one of the most potent combinations in NASCAR history.

*OFFICIALLY LICENSED BY* **NASCAR**

## Building The "Big'un"

In 1969, factory competition in NASCAR racing was at a fever pitch. Ford introduced the Talladega, while Chrysler countered with the Superbird. Hardly resembling stock family sedans, these automobiles quickly got the speeds up near the 200 mph mark. Coincidentally, Bill France had begun building his second dream- Talladega Superspeedway. It would be the biggest, fastest track in all of NASCAR racing.

### And You Think You Have Problems Handling A 42-Car Field...

The cars in the photo above are lining up at the back of the grid for the 1956 Daytona Beach Race. The starting field was comprised of seventy-six cars! In fact, the first Daytona 500 had a starting lineup of fifty-nine entrants, and some were convertibles. NASCAR finally began trimming the fields down in the mid-sixties, though the 1973 Talladega 500 did have sixty cars in the starting lineup! (Daytona Racing Archives)

150 *American History: The Evolution Of NASCAR Racing*

Looking back on the sixties, American stock car racing had launched a whole new market in the sports world, previously untapped. The predominantly southern crowd had long since shown the car makers that what was seen at the track would be bought at the dealership. But despite the facts, NASCAR was still without a major sponsor, until Junior Johnson put in a call to the R. J. Reynolds Company, seeking car sponsorship.

Reynolds had been looking for a marketing opportunity, but wanted something on a larger scale than flagging a car or two with their logos. They had looked into other possible outlets, but nothing seemed to fit. The opportunities were either too large to undertake, or too small to be deemed worthwhile.

**Blame It On The Bird**

In the late sixties and early seventies, the auto makers were going to some radical extremes to one-up the competition. Ford built the Talladega and Chrysler made the Superbird. NASCAR responded by instituting restrictor plates (devices that limit fuel flow into the engines) to bring these cars speeds down, ultimately leading to their demise. In the photo above, Pete Hamilton brings the Petty Enterprises Superbird in for service. (Daytona Racing Archives)

After carefully surveying all possible options, R. J. Reynolds formulated an aggressive game plan they would announce to the sporting community.

American History: The Evolution Of NASCAR Racing 151

## The New NASCAR

In 1970, the R. J. Reynolds Company signed on as NASCAR's chief sponsor. The sport was transformed, almost overnight. What was once the Grand National division now became known as the NASCAR Winston Cup division. RJR pumped money into a Winston Cup points fund and repainted some of the track walls red and white, Winston's colors.

## "I Gotta Have A V-8"

The brand new Talladega Superspeedway became a keystone of stock car speed in short order. On March 24, 1970, Buddy Baker became the first stock car driver to crack the 200 mph barrier when he turned in a closed course lap average of 200.447 mph. Eight months later, Bobby Isaac drove his Dodge to a 201.104 mph average, breaking Baker's record. Muscle cars were in, while the long sedans of the sixties were but a faded memory.

NASCAR closed a significant chapter of its history for good in September of that year. Richard Petty won the last Grand National race held on dirt when he took the checkered flag at the Homestate 200 in Raleigh, N.C. NASCAR had now acquired a full complement of speedways it could call its own, and with the RJR sponsorship coming on board, the image of American stock car racing was expanding.

# The Mantle Changes Hands

The sixties proved to be a decade of development, while the seventies became a decade of records and refinement. However, Bill France, Sr. would not be overseeing this transition; instead, his son Bill, Jr. would man the helm. Bill France, Jr. had grown up around NASCAR. He'd emptied the office trash, worked on the speedway maintenance crews and been involved in tense rules discussions. In 1972, after nearly a quarter of a century in the captain's chair, the elder France decided to retire. He tapped Bill Jr. to succeed him.

Bill France, Jr. had learned something important from his father: in order for the sport to remain vibrant, the competition had to be waged on a level playing field. That meant becoming the caretaker of NASCAR's rulebook, seeing to it that no single manufacturer could dominate another, week in and week out.

### The Privateers

NASCAR has always had its independents, the self-made individuals who somehow get by without the aid of a marquee sponsor's greenbacks. Raymond "Friday" Hassler, pictured above, was one such driver.

Hassler ran his operation with what he had. And if he didn't have it, he'd often invent it himself. Since Friday had no factory backing, he had to buy his own cars. Instead of buying an entirely new model each year, he'd simply replace items on his existing car, such as the quarter panels or other parts that the auto maker had restyled.

Friday died in 1972, but the privateers still live on. Dave Marcis is a current example of a successful "privateer." (Daytona Racing Archives)

American History: The Evolution Of NASCAR Racing  153

**OFFICIALLY LICENSED BY**

///////*NASCAR*.

# The Masters At Work

In the late sixties and early seventies, a handful of drivers emerged as the ones to beat. One of these drivers was likely to win on any given weekend, at any track. Lee Roy Yarbrough, Cale Yarborough, Richard Petty, Bobby Allison, Bobby Isaac and David Pearson claimed most of the checkered flags.

Later, the names of Buddy Baker, Donnie Allison and Darrell Waltrip could be mentioned along with this elite group. Of these, Lee Roy Yarbrough became the first NASCAR driver to be named American Driver of the Year; 1967 NASCAR Rookie of the Year Donnie Allison, driving for A. J. Foyt, finished fourth enroute to winning Rookie of the Year honors in the 1970 Indianapolis 500. Richard Petty would later record 200 career victories, David Pearson and Bobby Allison joined Petty in the million-dollar winner's club, and Bobby Isaac won races, retired, came back, and won some more.

David Pearson began racking up a winning percentage that was unheard of on the speedways. Known as the "Silver Fox" because of his crafty skill behind the wheel, Pearson drove for the Wood Brothers

### He Liked 'Em Big

Lee Roy Yarbrough was from Jacksonville, just 85 miles north of Daytona. In the late sixties, Yarbrough burst onto the NASCAR scene, as if out of nowhere. Driving Fords out of Junior Johnson's stable, he won 14 NASCAR races, drove in the Indy 500 and won American Driver of the Year honors in 1969. Lee Roy owned the big tracks in 1969, winning both events at Daytona, both at Darlington, and one each at Atlanta & Charlotte. (Daytona Racing Archives)

**154** *American History: The Evolution Of NASCAR Racing*

team in the seventies. He finished his career with 105 career NASCAR wins, second only to Richard Petty. Pearson was known as a smooth, patient driver who somehow found a way to get to the front when he needed to.

While Petty and Pearson had battled for supremecy in the early seventies, Cale Yarborough moved to the forefront in the mid seventies, picking up wins in chunks. He claimed three in a row at Martinsville and North Wilkesboro, but it can hardly be said that he favored the short tracks. After all, by the time he retired in 1988 Cale had won at least one race at every NASCAR track he competed on, including nine victories at Bristol alone. Yarborough also won three straight NASCAR Winston Cup Championships, 1976-78.

### Cale Yarborough: "Tough As Nails"

He was a two-time Golden Gloves Champ and High School All-State fullback. He tried to earn his living raising turkeys, lumberjacking, and performing auto and aerial stunts in a thrill show before his career as a driver took off. He wrestled alligators and bears, and played semi-pro football. Wherever there was a challenge, Cale Yarborough was right there in the thick of it.

Born William Caleb Yarborough, Cale entered his first NASCAR race at age seventeen by filing a false birth certificate. The year was 1957, and the race was, fittingly enough, the Southern 500 at Darlington. Yarborough was eventually found out and disqualified from the event.

Cale retired after the '88 season with the fifth most career wins (83) in NASCAR history, and still the only driver to win three straight Winston Cup Championships. He is now a successful businessman and NASCAR team owner. (Daytona Racing Archives)

*American History: The Evolution Of NASCAR Racing*

**Like A Hungry Wolfpack That Just Saw A Spare Rib:** Tight racing action like this is what NASCAR is all about. Richard Petty (43) sets up on the outside as the entire 1974 Daytona 500 field fills his rear-view mirror. Directly behind Petty are NASCAR greats Cale Yarborough (11), David Pearson (21) and Donnie Allison (88). Petty won the race with an average of 140.894 mph. It was his fifth Daytona 500 victory. Before he stepped out of the cockpit for good, he'd win two more. (Daytona Racing Archives)

Buddy Baker reached a major milestone in 1976, when he became the first NASCAR driver to complete a 500 mile race in less than three hours. Baker sped to victory in the Winston 500 at Talladega in two-hours, fifty-six minutes. It was his third win in a row at the Alabama speedway.

NASCAR's aggressive marketing program was beginning to pay dividends at this point. At the end of the year, a survey published by the Goodyear Tire and Rubber Company revealed that NASCAR Racing had taken the lead in worldwide fan attendance among auto racing events. Remember, this was before network television began airing major NASCAR events with any regularity!

*OFFICIALLY LICENSED BY*
*NASCAR*

# The Petty Legend

Before Richard Petty became known as "the king" in stock car racing circles, his father Lee won 54 NASCAR races. In fact, father Lee once protested a race against his son, and won.

To say that stock car racing is in Richard Petty's blood would be an understatement. His son Kyle won the very first NASCAR race he entered (the '79 ARCA Daytona event), becoming the first third-generation driver in NASCAR history to win a race.

Richard Petty wrote, rewrote and filled the NASCAR recordbook by the time he ended his brilliant career with a "Fan Appreciation Tour" in 1992: Seven Daytona 500 victories; NASCAR's first millionaire ('71); Seven Winston Cup Championships; The 27-win season of '67; and of course, his 200 career NASCAR wins.

Johnny Bruner, NASCAR's first starter, waves the checkered flag for Lee Petty. The elder Petty won the Daytona Beach race in 1954, and the first Daytona 500 in 1959. (Daytona Racing Archives)

*American History: The Evolution Of NASCAR Racing* 157

Appropriately enough, Richard Petty recorded his 200th win on July 4, 1984 at Daytona International Speedway. President Ronald Reagan was in attendance as Petty beat Cale Yarborough to the caution flag on the 157th of 160 laps. That day, Petty's Pontiac bore an engine prepared by Robert Yates.

In racing his way through NASCAR history, Richard Petty's name spans five decades (1958-1992). He racked up fifteen wins apiece at North Wilkesboro and Martinsville, eleven at North Carolina Motor Speedway, and ten at Daytona. His familiar number 43 was emblazoned on four different makes of Daytona 500 winners: Plymouth, Dodge, Oldsmobile and Buick. And, he was the first full-time NASCAR driver to break Dan Gurney's hold on the old Riverside road course.

Richard Petty has now retired, and owns a NASCAR team. His 200 wins and 27-win seasons (ten in a row!) are marks that will probably never be broken.

He's visited the White House, had streets named after him and signed thousands of autographs (he calls them "thank you notes"). All stock cars today even have a part named after him. The "Petty Bar," the part of the roll cage that runs from the right side of the driver's seat area to the top right corner of the cage. His father Lee is believed to be the first driver to use a full roll cage in his race car.

The Petty name currently has 261 NASCAR wins attached to it, counting father Lee and son Kyle. It is without question, the greatest name to have ever hung over a stock car driver's door.

OFFICIALLY LICENSED BY
///////NASCAR.

In 1979, CBS Television conducted the first live broadcast of the Daytona 500, in its entirety. Their most talented scriptwriters couldn't have created such a wild finish. On the final lap, Cale Yarborough attempted to pass Donnie Allison inside on the back straight. The two cars got tangled up and came to a crumpled, smoldering rest on the infield. Yarborough and Allison climbed out of their wrecks and began slugging it out as a national television audience looked on. Richard Petty streaked by for the victory, and Bobby Allison parked his car and climbed out to aid his younger brother. The television ratings for the last half-hour were exceptional. Daytona 500 viewers got to ride along with Yarborough via the in-car cameras for back-to-back wins in '83 and '84.

As the seventies drew to a close, one name had been seen near the top of the NASCAR Winton Cup Championship point standings with increasing regularity. That name was Darrell Waltrip. The Kentucky native was able to run with the best week in and week out, and in 1981 he won his first Winston Cup title. He successfully defended the title in 1982, and added a third championship in 1985.

Along with Darrell Waltrip, many of today's NASCAR stars began emerging in the early eighties. 1979 Rookie Of The Year Dale Earnhardt won his first NASCAR title in 1980, and has since averaged a NASCAR Winston Cup Championship every other year. Known as the "Intimidator" and "The Man In Black" because of his competitive driving style, Earnhardt reached the million-dollar winnings milestone in only his third full year driving on the NASCAR circuit.

Newcomers Bill Elliott, Ricky Rudd and Terry Labonte began easing out some of the seasoned veterans. More big money car sponsorships arrived with this influx of fresh talent.

**American History: The Evolution Of NASCAR Racing**

**OFFICIALLY LICENSED BY NASCAR**

Gone were the days of "Joe's Garage" painted across the rear quarter-panels. Instead, major corporations were recognizing the appeal of stock car racing, and the buying power that NASCAR fans wield.

Teams expanded their operations in areas of both equipment and personnel. Instead of a flatbed trailer bringing one or two cars to the track, NASCAR teams now had elaborate transport semi-trucks that not only carry two cars and many spare parts, but also have a detailed workshop inside. Some NASCAR Winston Cup teams of today own as many as ten cars for a single driver: two superspeedway cars, two short track cars, two road course cars, two spare cars and two cars under construction or in testing.

**Bobby**

**Donnie**

**Davey**

**Neil**

**The Alabama Gang**

Bobby, Donnie and Davey Allison, and Neil Bonnett. Together these four men put Hueytown, Alabama on the map. Bobby and Donnie are brothers; Davey was Bobby's son, and Neil was a close friend of the Allison family. Known by Hueytown citizens to be "down to earth, regular guys," they combined to win 132 NASCAR races. Davey died in 1993 following a helicopter accident; Neil Bonnett died in 1994. Bobby is a NASCAR Winston Cup team owner. (Daytona Racing Archives)

160 *American History: The Evolution Of NASCAR Racing*

# $ The Winston Million $

In 1985, R. J. Reynolds announced a new addition to its sponsorship package: "The Winston Million." The plan called for a million dollar bonus to be payed to any driver who could win three out of four races in the same year- The Daytona 500 (NASCAR's richest), The Winston 500 at Talladega (NASCAR's fastest), The Coca-Cola 600 at Charlotte (NASCAR's longest), and The Southern 500 at Darlington (NASCAR's oldest). In addition, RJR would pay a $100,000 bonus to the first driver who could win any two of the four in the same season.

# "Awesome Bill From Dawsonville"

It didn't take long for somebody to grab the cash RJR had posted. Bill Elliott won the Daytona 500, then won the Winston 500 at Talladega, driving the fastest 500-mile race in NASCAR history in the process. Elliott averaged 186.288 mph for the race!

Elliott had two of the four events in hand, and now it came down to the Southern 500 at Darlington. Cale Yarborough had the lead on his home track late in the race, but the power steering pump on his car failed Elliott was right there to snatch the win, and pocket a cool million.

Before the sun set on the season of '85, Bill Elliott had won more prize money in a single season than any other driver. Oddly enough, despite earning nearly $2.4-million in prizes, Elliott did not take home the NASCAR Winston Cup Championship. That award went to Darrell Waltrip instead.

**American History: The Evolution Of NASCAR Racing**

Waltrip wasn't simply handed the title, he had a great year himself. RJR had also arranged a race comprised of NASCAR Winston Cup race winners from the previous season, featuring a $500,000 payout. Called simply "The Winston," Darrell Waltrip won it; his season victory resume' also included wins at Charlotte, Richmond and Rockingham.

In the latter half of the eighties, NASCAR made changes in its road course schedule. The bankrupt, weed-choked Watkins Glen course was purchased by Corning, Inc., and the International Speedway Corporation. After an extensive refurbishing, the track was added to the Winston Cup schedule in 1986. Over 100,000 exuberant fans jammed the course to see the late Tim Richmond win the initial race from the pole. Later, the fabled road course at Riverside was turned into a housing community by land developers. NASCAR later added Sears Point Raceway to the schedule, ensuring the series of a yearly visit to California.

Rusty Wallace (27) leads Benny Parsons (55) and the rest of the 1986 Firecracker 400 field at Daytona. Wallace went on to finish eighth. (Daytona Racing Archives)

## Recent Developments

In 1992, Richard Petty hung up his helmet with 200 wins notched on it. The man known among stock car fans as "the king" is now focusing on a career as a NASCAR team owner.

In 1993, plans to stage a first-ever NASCAR Winston Cup race at the Indianapolis Motor Speedway were announced. Drivers began taking part in extensive practice sessions at the sacred oval, eagerly anticipating the race's August 1994 inception. King Richard himself even clocked a few hot laps around the speedway in one of his #43 Pontiacs, then promptly climbed out and donated it to the IMS Hall of Fame Museum.

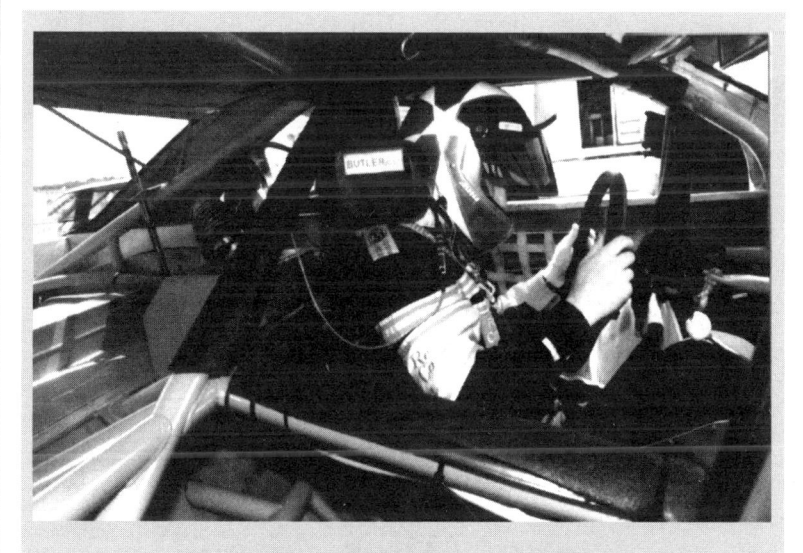

**An Inside Look At The Cars Of Today**

Elton Sawyer installs the removable steering wheel in his car. Behind Sawyer, the screw jacks extend upward through the rear window, facilitating wedge adjustments. The two thick hoses behind the driver's seat direct outside air into a reservoir that cools the differential, while the driver's helmet also receives ventilation piped inside the car. During a race, the interior of a stock car is likely to reach 140 degrees. Drivers must have extraordinary stamina to last 500 miles under these conditions. Interestingly enough, in the seventies researchers monitored driver David Pearson's vital signs during actual NASCAR Winston Cup races. Shockingly, they found that Pearson's pulse and blood pressure readings were lower when racing! (Courtesy of Campbell & Co.)

*American History: The Evolution Of NASCAR Racing* 163

**OFFICIALLY LICENSED BY NASCAR**

Dubbed "The Brickyard 400," the race was an instant drawing card- not only with fans, but with several famous drivers. IndyCar veterans Geoff Brabham and Danny Sullivan each qualified for the starting field. A. J. Foyt even came out of retirement to slide through the window of a Ford and make the race. Foyt's car wore 50, the same number he used throughout much of his Winston Cup career, which includes five victories. Three of Foyt's wins were scored at Daytona International Speedway: back-to-back wins in the Firecracker 400, and a victory in the 1972 Daytona 500.

The Brickyard 400 offered the richest NASCAR purse to date, over three million dollars, but the sheer prestige of competing in the inaugural race was enough to interest the world's top drivers.

Rick Mast won the pole; fittingly, it was his first ever. Ernie Irvan and young Jeff Gordon waged a fierce battle for the lead in the waning laps, but Irvan developed problems late in the race. Gordon, driving like a seasoned veteran, was able to maintain his lead, crossing the yard of bricks and claiming the victory.

## A Few Miles Ahead

Although it's already been said, NASCAR's history is extremely rich. So many colorful characters, so many exploits, so many great cars, so many great races...so few pages available to possibly list them all. Along the way, NASCAR's image has become a genuine force in the world of auto racing. Its drivers no longer hail from strictly the South, but rather from all over the country. In fact, NASCAR's roster of drivers includes women as well as men. Patty Moise and

Shawna Robinson have each set stock car speed records of over 215 mph! Robinson also became the first woman to win the pole in a NASCAR Busch Grand National race, doing so at Atlanta in 1994.

NASCAR racing has even had an impact on the U. S. Olympic Team. Driver Geoff Bodine designed a bobsled that many olympians feel presents a serious step toward the gold medal.

NASCAR racing has become one of America's most popular forms of sports entertainment. Each race weekend, crowds pack the grandstands to share in a euphoric rise of rpms. NASCAR's future miles promise to be fast, exciting and highly competitive. And to the talented people who'll drive those miles, we look forward to sharing the ride.

Left photo: Buddy Baker (15) dueling on the banks of Daytona with David Marcis (71). Right photo: Buddy stands in victory lane after another victory at Talladega. All in all, he took home the "winner's hardware" nineteen times. (Daytona Racing Archives)

American History: The Evolution Of NASCAR Racing

## Important! Read Before Painting

You must have a mouse with its driver installed in order to use the Paint Kit.

The NASCAR Racing **Paint Kit** allows you to create many different sets of cars, saving them under any name you wish. These **Car Sets** can then be loaded from within NASCAR Racing. **Car Sets** can store different collections of opponent cars, or contain several different paint schemes for your own car.

The original **Car Set** shipped with NASCAR Racing is called "`CARS94.DAT`." This file can be found in the `NASCAR\CARS\CARS94` directory. It is highly recommended that a new Car Set be created rather than painting the cars contained in the `CARS94.DAT` file.

To make a new car set, type **PAINTKIT** *filename*. For example, let's make a new **Car Set** called "CARS95." Be sure you are in DOS, and in the NASCAR directory before proceeding. Type PAINTKIT CARS95. The program will now search for a subdirectory called "CARS95." If it does not find one, it will ask you if you'd like to create one. Respond **"Yes"** to continue. Next, the program asks if you'd like to create the file called "CARS95.DAT". Once again, choose **"Yes."**

Note: The NASCAR\CARS\CARS94\CARS94.DAT path and filename must exist in order for the game to run; therefore, they should not be altered. If this path is corrupted, you must go back and re-install the game. It is a good idea to create a "dummy" directory (called "sets," for instance), and store a copy of the original CARS94.DAT file there for safe keeping.

Now that you've created a new car set to work with, you're ready to start painting. From the **Main Menu** of the Paint Kit, use your mouse to point to the **Paint Car** button in the lower left corner. Click the left mouse button once to choose **Paint Car**.

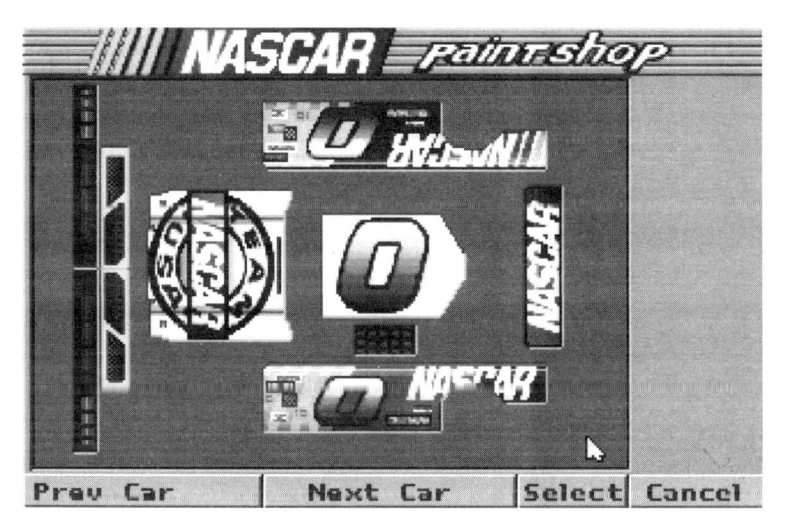

*Using The Paint Kit*

## Choosing A Car To Paint

The first car you see will be your own car. You can choose it, or you can paint any other car in the game. Use the left mouse button to click on **Prev Car** or **Next Car** to cycle through the list of available cars to paint. When you see the car onscreen that you want to paint, click on **Select**.

## The Decal Shop

Whether you've got a high-buck sponsor, or "Bill's Towing" backing your team, your car can be adorned with a variety of logos and styles. Use the Decal and Icon Libraries provided, or draw your own logos from scratch with the tool box. The Decal Shop contains special tools to facilitate placing and/or drawing graphics on your stock car's prepainted bodywork.

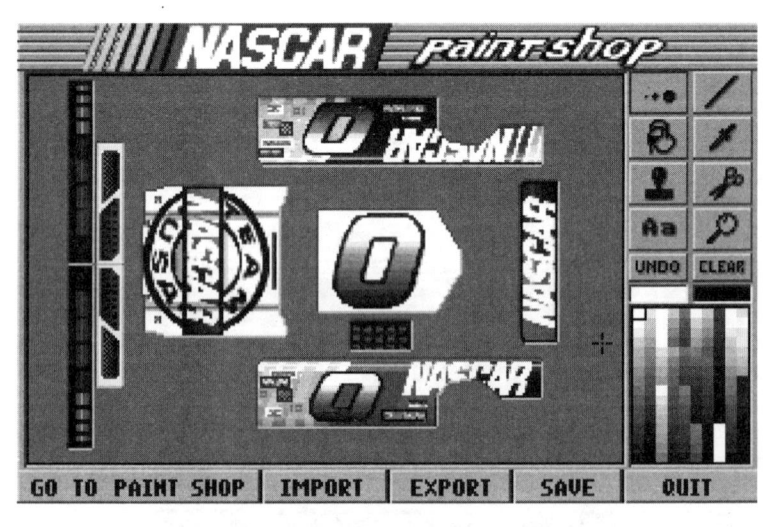

The Decal Shop consists of a parts window, tool box, color palette and command bar.

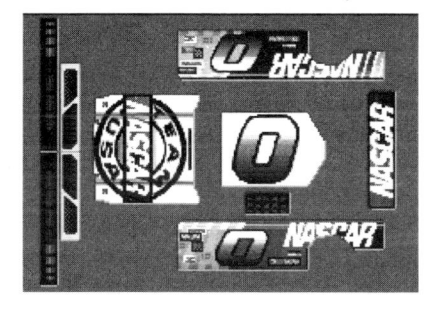

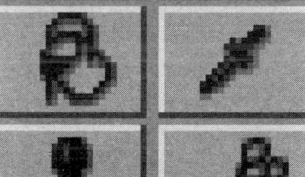

**The Parts Window:** Allows you to draw or apply existing logos, numbers, or other designs directly onto the body panels.

### The Tool Box

|  | | |  |
|---|---|---|---|
| Brush Type | | | Line Tool |
| Fill Tool | | | Get Color Tool |
| Stamp Tool | | | Cut Out Tool |
| Text Tool | | | Zoom In |
| Undo Button | UNDO | CLEAR | Clear Button |
| Main Color | | | Secondary Color |

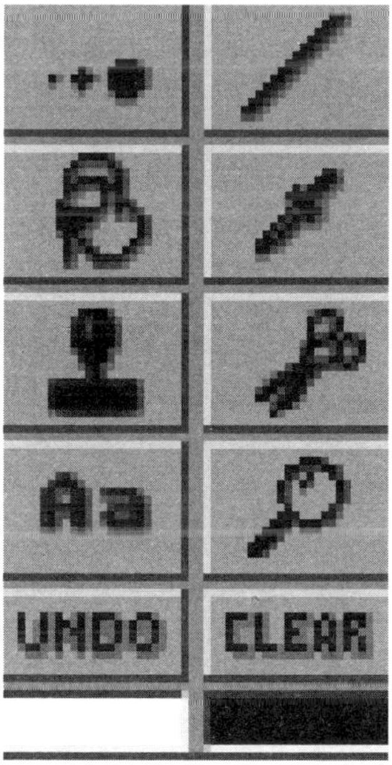

# Using The Tool Box

Using the left mouse button, point to and click on the tool you wish to use. The mouse cursor will change to reflect the shape of the tool currently active.

*Using The Paint Kit*

**OFFICIALLY LICENSED BY NASCAR**

**Brush Type:** Grab the paintbrush tool for some freehand drawing. Click the right mouse button on the **Brush Type** toolbox icon to open a window with different brushes inside. Choose the brush you wish to use, and begin drawing on any part by pressing and holding the left mouse button. Use the left mouse button to paint with the **Main Color**; use the right mouse button to paint with the **Secondary Color**.

**Line Tool:** Handy for drawing straight lines, this tool is selected with the left mouse button. Your lines can be a variety of thicknesses, depending upon the **Brush Type** chosen. Again, use the left/right buttons to choose colors.

**Fill Tool:** This tool makes painting large areas easy. Grab it by clicking the left mouse button on the **Fill Tool** icon in the toolbox. A single click over any part will fill every area bounded by a common color.

**Get Color Tool:** Use this icon to grab any color from a part inside the parts window. Click the left button to load the color and the **Main Color**. The right button loads the color to the **Secondary Color**.

**Stamp Tool:** Use this to stamp provided logos and decals on your stock car. Click the right mouse button on it to open up the **Decal Library**. Choose between **Large** and **Small** decal sizes. Click on the left or right arrow icons to see additional decals. Click on either **Flip** button to invert the decal horizontally or vertically. The **Rotate** button spins the decal in 90 degree increments for use at different angles. Drag the decal over the body panel you wish to stamp it on, and click the left mouse button to place it.

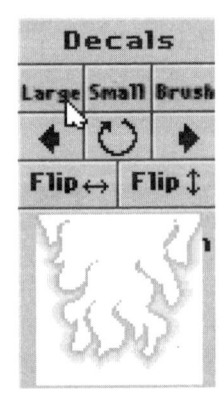

170　　　　　*Using The Paint Kit*

**Cut Out Tool:** This tool is a timesaver that makes recreating existing designs easy. Suppose you've drawn a design on the left rear quarter panel. You want that same design on the right rear quarter panel. Use the **Cut Out Tool** to grab the original design. Press and hold the left mouse button as you drag it across the existing design. Now, click the right mouse button on the **Decal Tool** icon, then choose **Brush** to manipulate the cut out image.

**Text Tool:** Click the right mouse button on the **Text Tool**. The **Rotate** button will spin the font in 90 degree increments. After choosing the orientation, left click on the body panel where you want to stamp it and type the desired letters on your keyboard. The color of the text is based on the color chosen in the **Main Color** box.

**Zoom In:** Click the left button over the magnifying glass to open a zoom window. Drag the window over the bodywork you wish to zoom in on, and left click. You can now edit the selected bodywork, pixel-by-pixel. Click the **Zoom In** tool again to return to the parts window.

**Undo:** Left click once to undo the most recent action.

**Clear:** Want to start with a clean slate? Left click once to clear all body panels of any paint or logo work.

**Main Color:** Use the left mouse button to draw or paint with this color. Select colors by positioning the cursor over the color palette and left clicking.

**Secondary Color:** Use the right mouse button to draw or paint with this color.

## Drawing Tips

You can easily draw matching or continuous lines that extend from one side of the car to the other. For example, using the Line Tool, left click on the driver's door. Holding the mouse button down, draw the line across the roof and to the matching spot on the passenger door. You can draw thicker lines or racing stripes by creating parallel lines of different widths and spacings. Come back later with the Fill Tool to change the colors of the stripes. Use the Decal Shop to draw body features on your car, such as hood pins, gas caps, vent ducts and front grills.

| GO TO PAINT SHOP | IMPORT | EXPORT | SAVE | QUIT |

## The Command Bar

Click on **Go To Paint Shop** to add base colors to the race car's body. Certain parts like the rear decklid and front fenders must be painted here. Use the **Import** button to bring previously exported car designs into the Paint Kit. The **Import** button works in conjunction with the **Export** feature to provide a means of saving individual designs outside of the CARS95.DAT file. This is handy when saving a work in progress. By **Exporting** your work, you can continue to drive the existing car until you finish your new design later. If the car you are working on is your own car, it will be saved with the filename "NASC0.PCX." If it was the Maxwell House car, it will be saved as "MAX22.PCX. The car number is always included in the exported filename. You can only import a file back onto the car it was exported from. Choose **Save** when you are ready to keep your final design. Choose **Quit** to return to the main **Paint Kit** menu.

## The Paint Shop

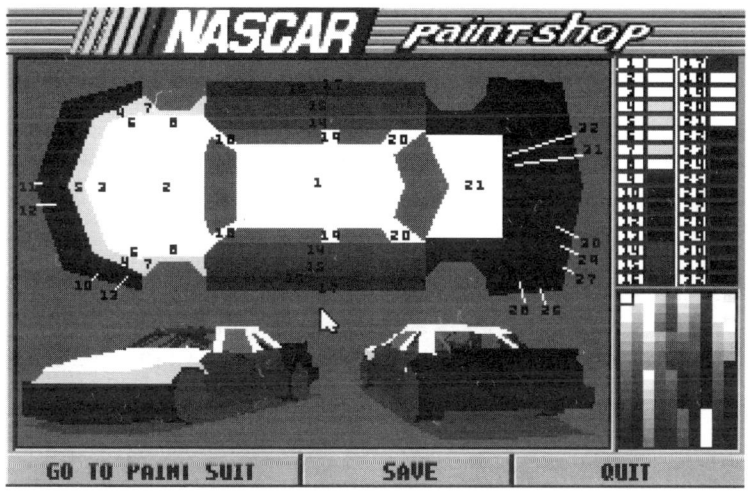

The Paint Shop features a collection of tools that allow you to choose the color schemes of the various panels that make up your stock car's bodywork. Each paintable location on the body is numbered for easy recognition. While most of the panels can be painted individually, some parts are painted in pairs. For example, if you paint part number 19 while, the opposite side automatically receives the same color. This helps ensure that both sides of your stock car will sport identical paint schemes.

The **Parts Window** displays a panel-by-panel depiction of the bodywork, as well as front and rear 3D profiles of the car. The window in the top right corner shows a color swatch beside each part's corresponding number. Beneath the swatch window you'll find the color palette, containing 160 hues. **Choose a color, then click the left mouse button on any piece of bodywork or in the swatch window to paint that part.**

*Using The Paint Kit* 173

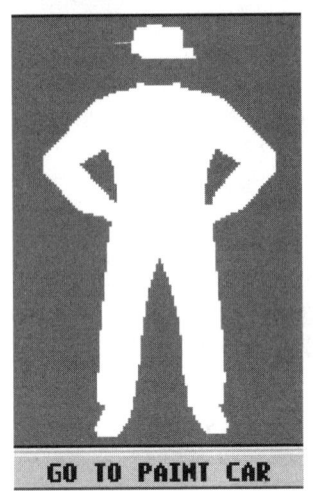

## Painting Uniforms

Click on Go To Paint Suit to custom design your crew members' uniforms. Painting suits is just like painting the car. Click on the swatch window, or directly on the part of the suit you wish to paint. Change uniform decal colors, stripes and hat colors to make your crew easier to spot when you're roarin' down pit road.

**Cut Out Tool Hint:** Use the **Cut Out Tool** to create multiple cars of the same design, such as teammates. For example, cut out the hood on the #71 Olive Garden car. Now, exit that car and select another car. Click the right mouse button on the **Stamp Tool**, and choose **Brush**. You can now paste the Olive Garden hood on the selected car.

## The Swap Cars Button

NASCAR Racing allows you to choose the number of opponents to race against, via the **Realism/Opponents Menu.** You could choose to race against fifteen opponents, but how do you pick the fifteen drivers you want to compete against? That's when the **Swap Cars** button is necessary. The Swap Cars button is located on the Command Bar of the Paint Kit's Main Menu.

The **Paint Kit** always opens the **Car Set** with the first car-yours. Using the **Prev Car/Next Car** buttons, you can move down the car list, in order. Since your car is at the top of the list, the last car you come to would be at the bottom.

Let's take an example: Suppose you want to race against twelve cars, and your favorite driver is Jeff Gordon. Before using the **Swap Cars** function, each time you enter a race Jeff's #24 DuPont Chevrolet is omitted. Click on **Swap Cars**, then continue to click **Next Car** until you see Jeff Gordon's car.

Now, click **Select**, then use the **Prev Car** button to move back up the car list, looking for an opponent you'd rather move down the list. When you find one, click **Select** again, and the two vehicles are swapped on the priority list. **You can swap as many cars as you like, with the exception of the first two. These are reserved for your car and the modem opponent.**

Note: The **Swap Cars** function does not swap driver's names, only car graphics. Using the **Driver Info Menu** in NASCAR Racing, or a word processor/text editor, you can change the driver's names by editing the file **"DRIVERS.TXT,"** found in the NASCAR/CARS/CARS94 directory. It may be helpful to jot down the car order you create within the Paint Kit, so you'll be easily able to match names with cars by creating this same order in the **DRIVERS.TXT** file.

# NASCAR WINSTON CUP
## 45 Years of Champions

| Year | Champion | Year | Champion |
|---|---|---|---|
| 1993 | Dale Earnhardt | 1971 | **Richard Petty** |
| **1992** | **Alan Kulwicki** | 1970 | Bobby Isaac |
| 1991 | Dale Earnhardt | **1969** | **David Pearson** |
| **1990** | **Dale Earnhardt** | 1968 | David Pearson |
| 1989 | Rusty Wallace | **1967** | **Richard Petty** |
| **1988** | **Bill Elliott** | 1966 | David Pearson |
| 1987 | Dale Earnhardt | **1965** | **Ned Jarrett** |
| **1986** | **Dale Earnhardt** | 1964 | Richard Petty |
| 1985 | Darrell Waltrip | **1963** | **Joe Weatherly** |
| **1984** | **Terry Labonte** | 1962 | Joe Weatherly |
| 1983 | Bobby Allison | **1961** | **Ned Jarrett** |
| **1982** | **Darrell Waltrip** | 1960 | Rex White |
| 1981 | Darrell Waltrip | **1959** | **Lee Petty** |
| **1980** | **Dale Earnhardt** | 1958 | Lee Petty |
| 1979 | Richard Petty | **1957** | **Buck Baker** |
| **1978** | **Cale Yarborough** | 1956 | Buck Baker |
| 1977 | Cale Yarborough | **1955** | **Tim Flock** |
| **1976** | **Cale Yarborough** | 1954 | Lee Petty |
| 1975 | Richard Petty | **1953** | **Herb Thomas** |
| **1974** | **Richard Petty** | 1952 | Tim Flock |
| 1973 | Benny Parsons | **1951** | **Herb Thomas** |
| **1972** | **Richard Petty** | 1950 | Bill Rexford |
| | | **1949** | **Red Byron** |

176

## A

Ace Setup 131-132
Acceleration 40-41, 117, 124, 130
Answer 36
Arcade Driving 51
Atlanta Motor Speedway 58-60, 132, 154
Automatic Braking 46
Automatic Shifting 46

## B

Ballast 102 *(see also Weight)*
Banking 127
Baud Rate 33-34
Bias 118, 123
  - adjustment 118-120
"Bluebird" 135
Bonneville Salt Flats 135-136
Bristol International Raceway 61-64, 86, 114-115
Bumping 91-92

## C

Camber 102, 107, 115-116
Cameras 25, 51-53, 55
Car
  - damage 43, 94
  - number 16
  - setup 33, 100-101, 131-132
    *(see Technical Setup)*
  - temperature 163
Car Sets 166-167
Championship Season 24, 29-31, 42-43
  - bonus points 30
  - NASCAR points 29
  - night races 43
  - player info 31
  - realism menu 31
  - saving a race 31
  - saving a season 31
  - schedule 29, 31
  - tires 99
Charlotte Motor Speedway 145, 154, 161
Chassis 39, 124-126, 140
  - adjustments 114
  - choices 39
Com Port 33, 38
Computer Connections 33-36
Contact Patch 98
Cornering 90-91
Cross Weight 118, 121-122 *(see also Wedge)*

## D

Damage Control 94
Darlington Raceway 65-67, 118, 139, 154, 161
Dashboard 7, 10, 14
Daytona 103, 133-135, 137-139, 147, 153-154, 162
  - Beach Race 136, 139, 141-143, 150
  - Daytona 500 143-145, 149, 156-159, 161
  - Firecracker 250 145
  - Firecracker 400 148, 162, 164
  - Int'l Speedway 143, 148, 158, 164
Delete
  - name & phone number 37
Description 37
Dial 36, 38
  - prefix 35
  - suffix 35
Differential 105
Direct Connect 34
Disk Utilities Icon 57
Done 28, 98
Downforce 88, 95, 107, 110, 113
Drafting 91-92, 105
Drivers
  - Allison, Bobby 154, 159-160
  - Allison, Davey 160
  - Allison, Donnie 154, 156, 159-160
  - Baker, Buddy 4, 152, 154, 156, 165
  - Beauchamp, Johnny 143
  - Bodine, Geoff 165
  - Bonnett, Neil 160
  - Byron, Red 138
  - Campbell, Sir Malcolm 135
  - Chupp, Obie 140
  - Cummings, Bill 137
  - DePalma, Ralph 135
  - Elliott, Bill 161
  - Foyt, A.J. 144, 154, 164
  - Goldsmith, Paul 143
  - Gordon, Jeff 164, 175
  - Hassler, Raymond "Friday" 153
  - Haugdahl, Sig 136-137
  - Isaac, Bobby 152, 154
  - Johnson, Junior 145, 151
  - Marcis, Dave 86, 120, 153, 165
    *Comments:*
    *Atlanta 59-60*
    *Darlington 67*
    *Michigan 73*
    *New Hampshire 74, 76*
    *Phoenix 79*

*Topical Index*

*Talladega  80, 82*
   *Watkins Glen  85*
 - Marion, Milt  103, 137
 - Moise, Patty  164
 - Oldfield, Barney  135
 - Owens, Cotton  143
 - Pearson, David  145, 154-156, 163
 - Petty, Lee  134, 143-144
 - Petty, Richard  60, 134, 145-146, 149, 152, 154-159, 163
 - Roberts, Glenn "Fireball"  143, 145
 - Robinson, Shawna  165
 - Sawyer, Elton  93, 163
 - Teague, Marshall  133-134, 140-141
 - Waltrip, Darrell  61, 154, 161-162
 - Weatherly, Joe  145
 - Yarbrough, Lee Roy  147, 154
 - Yarborough, Cale  61, 147, 154-156, 159, 161
Drag  110-113, 126
Drawing  45
Driver Info  24, 36, 39, 99
Driveshaft  105, 129-130
Driving Aids  10
   - menu  46
   - style  107

# E

Easy Setup  131-132
Edit Button  54
Engine Temperature  91-92, 94, 130
Error Correction  35
Error Detection  35
Exit  24

# F

Fast Setup  131-132
Ford  39
Frame Rate  48
France, Bill  137-139, 143-144, 150, 153
France, Bill Jr.  153
Front Air Dam  110-111, 113
Front Wheel Camber  115-116
Fuel  108-109
   - gauge  7
   - info  17
   - load  95, 97
   - octane  108
   - storage  109
   - summary  109
   - tank  14, 22, 109

# G

Garage  11, 26, 32, 36, 87-88
   - menu  96-97, 107, 111-112, 115, 125-126, 130-132
Gas Tank  19, 26
Gauges
   - fuel  7
   - current gear  7-8
   - oil pressure  7-8
   - oil temperature  7, 9
   - Speedometer  7
   - tachometer  7-9
   - water temperature  7-8
Gear Ratios  129-130
Gears  7-9, 97
Graphics  47-49
   - hot keys  48-49
   - improving game play speed  47
Groove  *(see Racing Line)*

# H

Heard  45  *(see also Sound)*
Hudson Hornet  133, 141, 144

# I

Indianapolis Motor Speedway  163-164
Initialization String  35-36, 38
Interval  12, 16
IRQ  33

# J

Joystick Use  25, 40-41, 53, 55-57

# K

Keyboard Shortcuts
   - arrows  5, 25
   - "C"  55
   - enter  5, 19, 56, 57
   - ESC  11, 23, 36, 52, 115
   - function  14-22, 51
   - less than/greater than  16-17, 19-21, 56-57
   - number keys  48-49
   - "P"  13-14
   - space bar  19, 56
   - "V"  55
Keyboard Use  41, 56

*Topical Index*

## L

Lap
- info 15
- pace 42-43
- projected laps 17
- remaining 12
- speed 12, 89

Linear Steering 41
Load 37, 132
"Loose" *(see Oversteer)*

## M

Main Menu 23-24, 32-33, 36, 39, 40, 41, 99, 167
Manual Shifting 10
Marcis, Dave *(see Drivers)*
Martinsville Speedway 68-70, 120, 129, 155, 158
Memory Management 54
Mileage 16
Michigan International Speedway 71-73
Modem Usage 32-35, 38
Mouse Usage 25, 166-175
Multiplayer Race 24, 32, 36-38

## N

Naming Your Team 39
NASCAR
- birth of 138-139
- drivers *(see Drivers)*
- schedule 29, 31
- tech ace *(see Tech Ace)*
- tracks *(see Tracks)*

Nelson, Gary 118
New Hampshire International Speedway 74-76, 87-88
Next Session 27, 36
Night Racing 43
Non-linear Steering 41
Number Of Opponents 36, 44

## O

Oil Pressure 7-9, 130
Oil Temperature 7, 9
Opponents Menu 44 45
Options 24, 131-132
- menu 31, 40, 46-47, 50
- garage menu 97, 131

Ormond Beach 135-137
Oversteer 88, 95, 120

## P

Pace Lap 42-43
Paint Kit 5, 25, 166-175
- command bar 172
- Decal Shop 168-171
- main menu 167, 172
- next car 168, 175
- paint car button 167
- painting uniforms 174
- parts window 169
- prev car 168, 175
- swap cars 174-175
- tips 172
- tool box 169
- tools 169-171
- Paint Shop 173

Passing 91-92
Pausing The Game 13
Phoenix International Raceway 77-79
Phonebook 37
Pitting 92-93
- pit board 11-12
- pit crew 14, 19-22, 174
- pit menu 112
- pit status 22
- pit stops 11, 17, 93-94

Place 12
Player Info 13, 99
Play/Pause 56
Points
- bonus points 30
- listing 29-31
- Winston Cup points 29-30

Pontiac 39
Pocition 12, 16
Practice 26-27 *(see Preseason Testing)*
Preseason Testing 6, 24, 27, 32
- menu 11, 53, 96

Projected Laps 17
"Push" *(see Understeer)*

## Q

Qualify 27

## R

Race 27
- menu 33, 96
- length 31, 42
- results 39

Race Weekend Menu 36
Racing Line 89-90, 127
Radio 13-15, 17, 19-22

*Topical Index*

Realism Menu  10, 27, 31, 42-43, 94
Rear Spoiler  *(see Spoiler)*
Rear View Mirror  9
Records  39
Replay  11, 25-26, 32, 36, 52-54, 56-57
   - delete  57
   - edit  54
   - load  57
   - play/pause  56
   - rewind  56
   - save  57
   - search/forward  57
   - search/rewind  56
Resume  11, 23
Rewind  56

# S

Saving
   - car sets  166
   - car settings  132
   - designs  172
   - name & phone number  37
   - race  28, 31
   - season  31
Screw Jacks  122, 163
Search/Forward  57
Search/Rewind  56
Select Camera  55
Select Car  55
Set Controls  40, 48
Shifting  91
Shocks  124-126
   - adjustments  87-88, 107, 124-126
   - stiffness  124-126
   - summary  126
   - therapy  126
"Shorter" Gear  130
Single Race  24, 26-27, 99
Sound, 50
Specify Modem  34-35
Speed  7, 107, 111, 113-114, 125-126, 129
Spoiler  9, 21, 97, 110-113, 126
   - adjustments  110-113
   - summary  113
Springs  102
Stagger  *(see Wheel Stagger)*
Standings  16, 28, 39
Steering  127-128
   - lock  88
Suspension  97, 114-116, 125-126
   - adjustments  102
   - camber  115-116
   - menu  117-118
Swap Cars  *(see Paint Kit)*

# T

Tachometer  7-10
Talladega Superspeedway  5, 6, 10, 80-82, 102, 120, 127, 129, 132, 150, 152, 156, 161
Talk Mode  36
"Taller" Gear  130
Technical Setups By Gary Nelson
   - Atlanta Motor Speedway  59
   - Bristol International Speedway  62
   - Darlington Raceway  66
   - Martinsville Speedway  69
   - Michigan International Speedway  72
   - New Hampshire International Speedway  75
   - Phoenix International Raceway  78
   - Talladega Superspeedway  81
   - Watkins Glen International  84
Testing  32
Textures  47, 49
Tires  98-107
   - adjustments  18
   - brands  31, 39, 99-100, 107
   - changes  19, 96
   - choosing  39
   - compounds  100
   - contact patch  98
   - grip  114, 124
   - inflation  103-104, 106
   - menu  104, 107
   - pressure  103-105, 107
   - "scuffs"  100
   - stagger  98, 105-106
   - "stickers"  22, 92
   - temperature  18, 91, 95, 101-104, 115-116, 122, 125
Tracks - *NASCAR RACING*
   - Atlanta Motor Speedway  58-60
      *setup list  59*
      *stats  58*
   - Bristol Int'l Raceway  61-64, 86
      *setup list  62*
      *stats  61*
   - Darlington Raceway  65-67
      *setup list  66*
      *stats  65*
   - Martinsville Speedway  68-70
      *setup list  69*
      *stats  68*
   - Michigan Int'l Speedway  59, 71-73
      *setup list  72*
      *stats  71*
   - New Hampshire Int'l Speedway  74-76, 87-88

*Topical Index*

   *setup list* 75
   *stats* 74
 - Phoenix Int'l Raceway 77-79
   *setup list* 78
   *stats* 77
 - Talladega Superspeedway 80-82
   *setup list* 81
   *stats* 80
 - Watkins Glen International 83-86
   *setup list* 84
   *stats* 83
Track Temperature 107
Transmission 129

## U

Understeer 87, 95, 109, 111, 122, 125

## V

VCR Command Bar 53-57
 - edit button 54

## W

Warm-up 27
Water Temperature 7-8
Watkins Glen International 162
Weather 42-43, 114
Wedge 20-21, 102, 117-118, 121-123
Weight 117-125
 - adjustments 87-88, 118-119, 123
 - ballast 118-120
 - cross weight *(see Wedge)*
 - transfer 124-125
Weight Jacking 107, 118, 123
Wheel Lock 127-128
Wheel Stagger 98, 105-107
Wheel/Yoke Usage 40-41
Winston Cup
 - championships 155-157, 159, 161
 - list of Champions 176
 - points 30
 - race 162-164
 - team 160
 - Winston 500 156, 161

## Y

Yellow Flags 16, 42-43

*Topical Index*

**OFFICIALLY LICENSED BY NASCAR**

### Designed By
*Adam Levesque*
*John Wheeler*
*David Kaemmer*

### Producer
*Adam Levesque*

### Lead Programmer
*John Wheeler*

### Programmers
*Dave Broske*
*Randy Cassidy*
*Richard Garcia*
*Charlie Heath*
*Jesse Hemmingway*
*David Kaemmer*
*Celso Minnitti*
*Dave Miller*
*Lisa Patacchiola*

### 3D Designers
*Matt Marsala*
*Dave Matson*
*Vladimir Starzhevskiy*
*Danny Walles*

### Art Director
*Sandro Carella*

### Artists
*Charles Bandes*
*David Flamburis*
*Brian Mahony*
*Doug McCartney*

### Marketing
*Ann-Marie Gianantoni*
*Laura Harlow*

**OFFICIALLY LICENSED BY NASCAR**

### Licensing Coordinator
Nicolette Heavey

### Quality Assurance
T. J. Fabrizio
Michael Gunthorp
Ed Martin
Jill Mironer
Jane Sieczkiewicz
Kenneth Swan

### Chief Test Driver
Matt Sentell

### Manual
Steve Vandergriff

### Sound Effects
Rob Wallace
Dennis Miller

### Music
Intro Riff By Rachel Bolan and Dave "Snake" Sabo
of Skid Row

MIDI Music: The Fat Man
Composer: Joe McDermott

**Special Thanks To:** All our dedicated beta testers, Charlie Cooper and NASCAR, Ned Jarrett, Gary Nelson, Dave Marcis, Joe Nemechek, Elton Sawyer, Patty Moise, Bob Weeks, Stephen Senappe, Jack Zinkan, Riggins Competition Motorsports, Bob, Jon and Linda at the Daytona Racing Archives, the folks at HMI, Emmett Byrd of the Atlanta Motor Speedway, and all of our significant others for their patience and love.

**Neil Bonnett 1946-1994**

**Get Well, Ernie!**

**OFFICIALLY LICENSED BY NASCAR**

## COPYRIGHT NOTICES

AC Delco is a registered trademark of Delco Electronics Corp. Division, General Motors Corporation. Auto Palace is a trademark of ADAP, Inc. Bosch is a registered trademark of Robert Bosch Co. BR DeWitt is a registered trademark of BR DeWitt, Inc. CARQUEST is a registered trademark of CARQUEST. Champion spark plugs is a registered trademark of Cooper Industries, Inc. Chevrolet, the bow tie emblem, Lumina and related body design are trademarks of the Chevrolet Motor Division, General Motors Corporation and used with permission to Papyrus Design Group, Inc. Dimension Cable is a trademark of Dimension Cable, Inc. DuPont is a registered trademark of DuPont Automotive Products, E.I. du Pont de Nemours and Company. Food City is a trademark of K-V-A-T Food Stores. Ford, the Ford emblem, Ford Racing, Ford Motorsports, and Thunderbird are registered trademarks of Ford Motor Company used under arrrangement by Papyrus Deisign Group, Inc. Fram Filters is a registered trademark of Allied Signal, Inc. Georgia Lottery is a trademark of the Georgia Lottery Corporation. Goody's is a registered trademark of Goody's Manufacturing Corporation. Goodyear (& winged foot design) and Eagle are trademarks of The Goodyear Tire & Rubber Co., reproduced by permission. Hoosier is a registered trademark of Hoosier Racing Tire reproduced by permission. Hooters is a registered trademark of Hooters of America, Inc. Jesse Jones Hot Dogs is a registered trademark of Goodmark Foods, Inc. Kendall Motor Oil is a registered trademark of Witco Corporation. Kroger is a registered trademark of Kroger Food Stores. MAC Tools is a registered trademark of Mac Tools, Inc. MBNA America is a federally registerd sevice mark of MBNA America Bank, N.A. MasterCard is a registered service mark of MasterCard International, Inc., used pursuant to license. This credit card offer is a cooperative marketing effort of MBNA America Bank, N.A. and NASCAR. MAXX Race Cards is a trademark of J. R. MAXX, Inc. Mobil 1 is a registered trademark of Mobil Corporation. Monroe is a trademark of Monroe Auto Equipment Co., subsidiary of Tenneco Inc. NATIONSCREDIT is a trademark of NationsCredit Corporation. PPG and the PPG emblem are registered trademarks of PPG Industries, Inc. and used under license by Papyrus Design Group, Inc. PEPSI and Pepsi emblem are registered trademarks of PepsiCo, Inc. Pontiac, Pontiac "Arrowhead" Emblem, Grand Prix, and Firebird Emblem are trademarks of General Motors Corporation used under license by Papyrus Design Group, Inc. Purolator is a registered trademark of Purolator Product, Inc. Rain-X and teardrop mark is a registered trademark of Unelko Co. Slick 50 is a registered trademark of Slick 50 Products Corporation. Somerville Lumber and arrow emblem are trademarks of Payless Cashways. STIHL is a trademark of Mid Atlantic STIHL Corp. SPRINT Cellular is a registered trademark of Sprint Corporation. TrueValue Hardware is a registered trademark of Cotter & Company. Valvoline registered trademark used with permission from the Valvoline Company, a division of Ashland Oil, Inc. Zippo is a registered trademark of Zippo Manufacturing Company.

OFFICIALLY LICENSED BY

///////NASCAR.

Darlington Raceway, Talladega Superspeedway and Watkins Glen International are registered trademarks of The International Speedway Corporation. Bristol International Speedway is a registered trademark. Phoenix International Raceway is a registered trademark. The track names and track likenesses of Darlington Raceway, Talladega Superspeedway, Watkins Glen International, Bristol International Speedway and Phoenix International Raceway are officially licensed by NASCAR Properties. The Atlanta Motor Speedway is a registered trademark, the mark and track likeness are used under license from the Atlanta Motor Speedway. Martinsville Speedway is a registered trademark, the mark and track likeness are used under license from Martinsville Speedway. Michigan International Speedway is a registered trademark of Penske Corporation, the mark and track license are used under license from Penske Corporation.

Rick Mast's name and the likeness of the #1 car, including Precision Products logo used under license with Precision Products and Rick Mast. Rusty Wallace's name and the likeness of the #2 car, including the Ford Motorsport logo are registered trademarks used under license with Penske Corporation. Sterling Marlin name and likeness and KODAK, GOLD and Trade Dress are trademarks licensed to Papyrus Design Group, Inc. by Eastman Kodak Company. The right to use the name, likeness and image of the Kellogg's Racing Team and Terry Labonte's name in association with Kellogg's Corn Flakes Racing Team are used under license with Wilson Marketing for the Kellogg's Corn Flakes #5 Hendrick Motorsport Chevrolet and for Terry Labonte, as agent for the Kellogg's Corn Flakes #5 Hendrick Motorsports Chevrolet. The name of Mark Martin and the likeness of the #6 Roush Racing car are used under license from Valvoline for the Licensed Product and related materials as directed by Valvoline. Geoff Bodine's name and the likeness of the #7 car including the Exide Batteries trademark are used under license with GEB, Incorporated. The name of Jeff Burton and the likeness of the #8 car including the trademark Raybestos Brakes are used under license with Stavola Bros. Racing Team. The likeness of the #12 car including the trademarks of Straight Arrow are used under license with Bobby Allison Motorsport. Family Channel trademark usage by authority of Roush Racing, Livonia, MI. Ted Musgrave's name and /or likeness by authority of Roush Racing, Livonia, MI. Loy Allen Jr.'s name and the likeness of the #19 car used under license with Hooters of America. The name and marks of CITGO are a registered trademark of CITGO Corporation. The name, marks and race car design of Wood Brother #21 car are used under license with CITGO Petroleum Corporation. The name of Bobby Labonte, the name and marks of the Maxwell Houe Coffee Compnay, and the name, marks and race car design of Bill Davis Racing are used under license with Advantage Management, Inc. The name of Jeff Gordon, the name and marks of DuPont Automotive Finishes, and the name, marks and race car design of Hendrick Motorsport, whether registered or unregistered, are used under license from Motorport Traditions, DuPont, Jeff Gordon and Hendrick Motorsports. The name of Ken Schrader is used by permission of Schrader Racing. The name of Brett Bodine, the name, marks and race car design of King Racing's #26 car, including the trademark of Quaker

**OFFICIALLY LICENSED BY NASCAR**

State Corporation, are used under license with King Racing. The name of Michael Waltrip, the name, marks and race car design of Bahari Racing's #30 car including the trademark of Pennzoil Company, are used under license with Bahari Racing and Michael Waltrip. The name of Ward Burton is used under license with Ward Burton. The name, marks and race car design of A.G. Dillard Motorsports' #31 car, including the trademark, Hardees, are used under license from Hardee's Food Systems, Inc. The name of Harry Gant is used under license with Harry P. Gant. The name, marks and race car design of Leo Jackson Motorsport's #33 car are used under license with Leo Jackson Motorsport. The name and likeness of Joe Nemechek are used under license with Nemco Motorsports. The name, likenesss and marks of Larry Hedrick Motorsports' #41 car, including the trademark, Meineke Muffler, are used under license with Larry Hedrick Motorsports. The name of Jimmy Hensley and the name, likeness and marks of the #55 RaDiUs Motorsports car, including the trademarks of Petron Plus, are used under license with RaDiUs Motorsports, Inc. The name and likeness of Dave Marcis and the name, marks and race car design of the #71 Marcis Auto Racing car, including the trademark, The Olive Garden, are used under license with Marcis Auto Racing. The name of Mike Wallace is used under license with Keystone Sports & Event Marketing, agent for Mike Wallace. The name, likeness and race car design of Donlavey Racing including the trademarks of Heilig-Meyers Company are used under license with Keystone Sports & Event Marketing.

Universal VESA TSR, Copyright ©1993 Kendall Bennett

LHA ©Haruyasu Yoshizaki, 1988-91.

Copyright ©1994 Bolan & Sabo.

Procomm is a registered trademark of Datastorm Technologies, Inc.

Telix is a registered trademark of EXIS, Inc.

Window's Terminal is a registered trademark of Microsoft Corporation.

**OFFICIALLY LICENSED BY NASCAR**

## Technical Support Information

If you are having difficulty installing the software, please consult the installation instructions. If you have a modem, you may also call our bulletin board service, 24-hours a day, seven days a week. The BBS provides a forum for players to swap car setup tips, discuss pit notes, or download new files and utilities as they become available.

Please try our bulletin board, fax or other online sources for the fastest customer service. For a free CompuServe membership and a $15.00 usage credit, call CompuServe at 1-800-524-3388, or 1-614-457-0802, and ask for operator 539. If you need further assistance with this product, you may call our technical support hotline, **Monday through Friday, 9am to 5pm Eastern Time.** Please be at your computer when you call, and be ready to describe your system's configuration in detail.

| | |
|---|---|
| **Papyrus Tech Support:** | (617) 868-3103 |
| **Papyrus BBS:** | (617) 576-7472 |
| **Papyrus Fax:** | (617) 349-3999 |
| **CompuServe Forum:** | **GO PAPYRUS** |
| **CompuServe Address:** | 72662, 2150 |
| **Internet:** | papyrus@world.std.com |
| | **(no spaces, all lower case)** |
| **Anonymous FTP:** | ftp.std.com, ftp/vendors/papyrus |

## LIMITED WARRANTY

Papyrus Design Group, Inc. warrants that the disks in this package will be free from defects in materials and workmanship under normal use for a period of ninety (90) days from the date of original purchase.

If within 90 days of purchase the disks prove defective, you may return the disks along with proof of purchase, your name, your address, and a description of the defect to:
Customer Service, Papyrus Design Group, Inc., 35 Medford Street, Somerville, MA 02143.

Papyrus Design Group, Inc. will replace the disks free of charge.

To replace the defective disks after the 90-day warranty period, send all of your original disks to the above address along with your name, your address, a description of the defect and a check or money order for $10.00/U.S.

## WARRANTY DISCLAIMER

WE DO NOT WARRANT THAT THIS SOFTWARE WILL MEET YOUR REQUIREMENTS OR THAT ITS OPERATION WILL BE UNINTERRUPTED OR ERROR-FREE. WE EXCLUDE AND EXPRESSLY DISCLAIM ALL EXPRESS AND IMPLIED WARRANTIES NOT STATED HEREIN, INCLUDING THE IMPLIED WARRANTIES OF MERCHANTABILITY AND FITNESS FOR A PARTICULAR PURPOSE.
Some states do not allow the exclusion of implied warranties, so the above exclusion may not apply to you. This limited warranty gives you specific legal rights, and you may also have other legal rights, which vary from state to state.

## LIMITATION OF LIABILITY

OUR LIABILITY TO YOU FOR ANY LOSSES SHALL BE LIMITED TO DIRECT DAMAGES, AND SHALL NOT EXCEED THE AMOUNT YOU ORIGINALLY PAID FOR THE SOFTWARE. IN NO EVENT WILL WE BE LIABLE TO YOU FOR ANY INDIRECT, SPECIAL, INCIDENTAL, OR CONSEQUENTIAL DAMAGES (INCLUDING LOSS OF PROFITS) EVEN IF WE HAVE BEEN ADVISED OF THE POSSIBILITY OF SUCH DAMAGES.
Some jurisdictions do not allow these limitations or exclusions, so they may not apply to you.

## NOTICE

The enclosed software program and this user manual are copyrighted. All rights are reserved. This manual may not be copied, reproduced, translated or reduced to any electronic medium or machine-readable form, in whole or in part, without prior written consent of Papyrus Design Group, Inc. The enclosed software program may be copied, by the original purchaser only, as necessary for use on the single computer for which it was purchased.